Know your child's IQ

7SP

D1743544

Professor Hans Eysenck

and

Darrin Evans

Acknowledgements

The authors and publishers wish to give their sincere thanks to the masters and pupils at Sevenoaks School, Dulwich College and the various other schools that co-operated with us to make the IQ conversions possible.

Published by Mind Games, 1995

©   Professor Hans Eysenck and Darrin Evans 1995

ISBN   1 899368 04 3

Contents

Introduction

Dear Parent,

Like most parents, we are sure, you have the best interests of your child very much at heart. One of the most troublesome areas of concern for most parents is undoubtedly that of education. It is universally recognised that education is extremely important, both from the point of view of helping to produce a knowledgeable, appreciative, competent human being, and from the point of view of helping the child to acquire sufficient marketable knowledge to go to university, get a good job, and quite generally get on in life. Both points of view are important. Good education is worthwhile in itself, in producing a well balanced person who appreciates what culture can give him or her in the fields of music, literature, painting, drama and science. But let us not despise the more utilitarian products of education; to obtain a reasonable job and to be able to read and write properly, be numerate, perhaps know one or two foreign languages, know how to present himself or herself to the best advantage, and show ability in several important commercial skills — computer science, for instance.

The commercial importance of education is shown very clearly in one simple figure: on average, every year of a child's education raises the average salary of a person by 16%! Thus education pays both ways — it helps make you a better person, more cultured, more knowledgeable in the ways of art and science, and it helps you get a better job, with better pay, better prospects and better working conditions. Note the 'average' above; education will not help you very much if you are an alcoholic, if you are severely neurotic or psychotic, if you have severe character faults, or if you have poor motivation or poor health. On the other hand, poor education does not prevent certain classes of people from achieving great worldly success — footballers, entertainers, sports men and women, prostitutes, models, film stars etc. But for 90% of the population at least, education is probably the most important factor in shaping their future lives.

In determining a person's likelihood of being successful in this quest for education, the most important single determinant is the IQ — the intelligence quotient. Of course other factors also count — the quality of the school, the interest taken by the parents, and the readiness of the child to work hard. But consider just one recent experiment. It was carried out on the Isle of Wight, where every child of five years of age was tested with an IQ test; in other words they used pre-school children who had not received any organised form of education at the time of testing. They were retested eleven years later, i.e.after finishing school, and their school achievements were noted. What was the outcome? The original IQ measure predicted with great accuracy how well they did in their final examination. It also predicted with great accuracy their final IQ, i.e.the one recorded at age 16. The school made no contribution to the IQ and school did little to determine scholastic success *independently* of IQ. What the child brought into the school system determined very largely what he or she took away from school. This fact has been emphasised again and again in hundreds of studies. It shows vividly how important IQ testing can be if you want to know the scholastic ability of your child.

It also indicates the silliness of publishing lists of different schools, noting their successes and failures; such tables have little meaning unless they correct the outcome tables by taking into account the quality of the intake! A school where the average IQ of the boys and girls entering it is 95 cannot compete with schools where it is 125, any comparison between them is nonsensical unless we correct the 'achievement' figures for potential IQ. For a child with an IQ of 85 to obtain an 'O' level is a remarkable achievement for the school; for a child with an IQ of 130 to obtain a number of 'A' levels is par for the course, unless the school is very inefficient. Yet schools and governments are so afraid of even mentioning the dreaded word 'intelligence' that this fact has completely escaped notice.

What is the IQ?

We generally distinguish in psychology 'cognition' from 'emotion'; cognition is the mental act or process by which knowledge is acquired, while emotion relates to moods, feelings and the like. Mental testing from the beginning concerned itself mainly with cognition, trying to measure a person's ability to acquire knowledge and his success in doing so. It was Alfred Binet, a French psychologist and educationalist, who produced the first proper intelligence tests. He based himself on a well known phenomenon, namely the simple fact that as a child gets older, he or she can succeed with the solution of more and more difficult problems. This gave him the idea of measuring the child's *mental age*, (MA). Take a problem that the average 6-year old can do:

   3   5   7   9   11   ?

The average 5-year old cannot find the answer to this simple progression, but the average 6-year old can. Take hundreds of different problems, give them to thousands of children, and discover at what age the average 5-year old, 6-year old, 7-year old etc can do each problem; then construct a *scale* going from the simplest test a 5-year old can do, to the most difficult, which only a 16 year old can do. If you now want to know how bright a child is, give him the whole set of items, and see how well he or she does with the items at any age level. Suppose there are six items at each age-level, and the child succeeds with all those at the 5, 6, 7 and 8-year old level, plus three items at the 9-year old level. The mental age of the child would be 8½, because he or she gets all the 8-year old items right, plus half the 9-year old ones. Thus we can establish a child's MA independently of the child's chronological age (CA).

The IQ test was introduced later to bring MA and CA together. If a child has an MA *higher* than his or her CA, the child is obviously brighter than average; if the MA is *lower* than the CA, the child is less bright than average. The formula generally used is IQ = (MA ÷ CA) × 100; you multiply by 100 to get rid of the decimal point. Thus if two 10-year olds have mental ages of 12 and 8 respectively, their IQs will be (12 ÷ 10) × 100 = 120, and (8÷10) × 100 = 80 respectively.

What does such an IQ mean? Figure 1 shows the distribution of IQs in the general population. Twenty-five percent will lie between 90 and 100, another 25 percent between 100 and 110. The mean of course is 100 (by definition), and half the population has IQs between 90 and 110; we may regard these as the *average* as far as intelligence is concerned. The higher (or lower) the IQ, the fewer people will be having that IQ. Thus only 4 children in a thousand have IQs above 140; and 2 in a hundred have IQs between 130 and 140. Consider this figure carefully; the position of your child on it can be very important for his or her educational future.

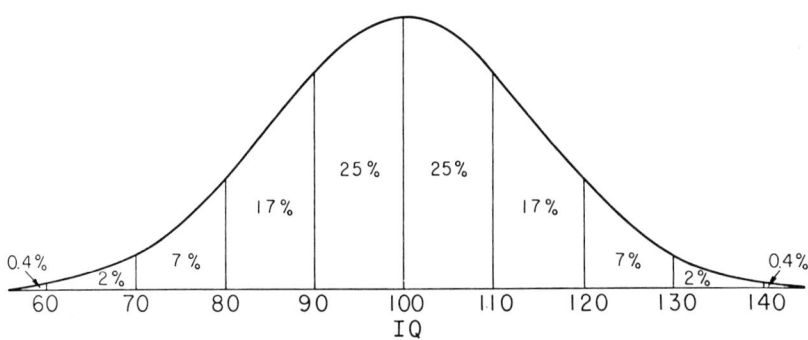

Figure 1: The distribution of IQs in the population

Some rough indications of the meaning of different IQs for different professions may be useful. University students will average 115 to 120; PhD students 130 or thereabouts. Top civil servants, university professors, leading businessmen and such will be 130 or above for the most part, and often above 140. Table 1 shows the mean IQ values for a variety of jobs; remember that these are only averages, so that many people in each group will have IQs higher or lower than the average. There is one observation in particular that is important in this connection: high IQ is a *necessary* but not a *sufficient* condition for the higher class of occupation. To be an accountant or a lawyer you *must* have a reasonable IQ, but you may have a reasonable IQ, but because of laziness or for some other reason, fail to use it to the best advantage. In the semi-skilled working class occupations you will find a wider range of IQs than in the middle class occupations; in other words, some of the miners, barbers and labourers will have quite high IQs, but hardly any of the teachers, auditors and chief clerks will have a low IQ! Look at the column in Table 1 marked S.D. This is a statistical term (standard deviation) measuring the *spread* of the IQs around the mean for each group; you will see that the spread increases from top to bottom by about 100%! Brightness, though essential, clearly is not enough to land a high class job; other things are required, such as application, motivation and luck!

You sometimes hear critics say, sneeringly, that all the IQ tells us is that the child is good at doing IQ tests. Clearly, that is nonsense. The IQ tells us how well your child is likely to do at school, and possibly at University; it also tells you the likely type of job the grown-up will find. If you were restricted to being told just one thing about a person, and asked to predict his or her future, nothing would be more predictive than an IQ. But of course, one must qualify this statement: IQ is not

Profession	Mean	SD	
Accountant	128	11.7	
Lawyer	128	10.9	
Auditor	125	11.2	
Reporter	124	11.7	
Chief clerk	124	11.7	**Middle class**
Teacher	122	12.8	**occupations**
Draughtsman	122	12.8	
Pharmacist	120	15.2	
Book-keeper	120	13.1	
Toolmaker	112	12.5	
Machinist	110	16.1	
Foreman	110	16.7	
Airplane mechanic	109	14.9	
Electrician	109	15.2	**Skilled working**
Lathe operator	108	15.5	**class occupations**
Sheet metal worker	108	15.3	
Mechanic	106	16.0	
Riveter	104	15.1	
Painter, general	98	18.7	
Cook & baker	97	20.8	
Truckdriver	96	19.7	
Labourer	96	20.1	
Barber	95	20.5	
Lumberjack	95	19.8	
Farmhand	91	20.7	
Miner	91	20.1	
Teamster	88	19.6	

Table 1: Mean IQ of people in different jobs

everything, not even as far as intelligence is concerned. For actual life success, personality, emotions, drive, mental health and many other factors are important and should never be forgotten. This does not diminish the importance of the IQ; it merely serves to set it in context.

Before turning to a consideration of some problems, in mental measurement generally, let us say one more thing about the IQ. Originally it was introduced in 1911 by William Stern (Binet never liked the concept) as an actual quotient, but it soon became clear that there were some problems connected with it. To be useful, clearly it requires that mental age increases in a linear fashion with chronological age, which it does quite satisfactorily from 5 to 16. But after that age (roughly) there is little growth in MA, and none after 20; that means that if we use the formula for adults IQ would fall as a person gets older! Take an average person, with an IQ of 100 at the age of 20: [(20÷20) × 100]. At the age of 40 it would be something like (20 ÷ 40) × 100 = 50, at the age of 80 it would be (20÷80) × 100 = 25! Clearly this is nonsense, and nowadays we measure the IQ in quite a different manner.

Look back at Figure 1. Instead of plotting the distribution of IQs, we could plot the distribution of scores on our test, i.e.the number of test items successfully solved. The distribution would look very similar, with most scores clustered around the mean, gradually tapering off in an orderly fashion towards the extremes. What we can now do, roughly speaking, is to identify an *average*, score with an IQ of 100, a score 25% above the mean with an IQ of 110 etc. Thus nowadays the IQ is no longer a quotient at all (even for children); it is determined by a statistical transformation which retains the central meaning of a measure of intelligence, but gets rid of the actual working out of a quotient. For parents the way these statistics are worked out is not important, but for the sake of clarity we should explain just how the IQ is determined nowadays.

One intelligence or many intelligences?

From the beginning of intelligence testing, there were two opposed views. One, represented by Sir Francis Galton, regarded intelligence as a single, universal ability to do well with any kind of cognitive problem; this ability, he thought, was largely innate, and determined by biological properties of the nervous system. Binet, on the other hand, thought of intelligence as just the sum, or average, of a number of quite distinct abilities — verbal, numerical, spatial, memory, etc; these, he thought, would be profoundly affected by teaching and other environmental factors. I shall deal later on with the question of nature versus nurture; as one might have surmised, both are involved — indeed, it is meaningless to imagine differences in IQ or personality or anything else being determined *exclusively* by either heredity or environment. Similarly, in the case of the one or the many, both men were right in what they asserted, and wrong in what they denied.

What is the evidence in favour of Galton? Imagine that you have asked 1,000 psychologists to draw up 100 IQ problems each, problems that express their private views of the nature of intelligence. Imagine you have administered all the resulting problems to 10,000 children, and now look at the results. What would Galton predict? He would expect that children who did well with *any* kind of problem would also do well with all the other types; conversely, children who did not do so well with one kind of problem would also fail to do well with all other kinds. In other words, there would be good agreement as to a child's capacity between all different types of problems. This is indeed what is always found, regardless of type of problem, age or sex of child, country or race — we always find what is technically known as a *positive manifold*. So Galton seems to be right.

But wait! In addition to this general ability, often written as '*g*', we also find that certain types of problem tend to go together. Some children are better on problems involving *words*, others at problems involving *numbers*, or *spatial* configurations, or *memory* processes —in other words, in addition to '*g*' or general intelligence we have special abilities, like those mentioned above. Thus Binet was right too — there are special and separate abilities. The general picture of intelligence now universally accepted is a hierarchical one — a number of special abilities, some 20 in number, all correlate with each other, in defining a general concept of *intelligence* encompassing all the special abilities.

How do we select the items that go together to make up an IQ test? We can do one of two things.

1   We can select items that define '*g*' most closely, and eliminate items that measure special abilities to any marked extent.

2 We can select items measuring all the abilities that have been recognised, and take an average of all the individual scores on the special tests. Both types of testing have been done, and they give almost identical results — as indeed they should! But method 1 in practice is easier, and needs far fewer test items; consequently it is usually preferred unless we also want to know about the special abilities which can be important in identifying areas of special competence. However, IQ tests used for selection purposes in schools usually prefer the first method of item selection, and that has in the main been followed in this book.

Given this method of test construction, how do we choose the types of item? Over the years, we have learned what sort of item gives us the best estimates of a child's IQ, and this knowledge is based on complex statistical analyses of thousands of items, done by hundreds of thousands, if not millions, of children and adults. These analyses are based on *correlations*, and a brief discussion of this concept may be useful; it enters into everything we shall discuss later. Suppose you are knowledgeable about football, and write down your prediction, about which team will be first, second, third etc in the premier league next year. How can you compare your prediction, and its accuracy, with the prediction made by a friend, or by a journalist, in the sports pages of a newspaper? You calculate a *correlation*, which gives you a value of 1.00 if your prediction is perfectly correct, and a value of 0.00 if it bears no relation at all to the eventual ranking. Such predictions tend to result in correlations of around 0.60, and if yours is higher than your friend's, or the journalist, then you win!

Returning to our tests done by thousands of children, we can take the tests and write down the scores of all our children; we can then calculate *correlations* between the tests. The higher the correlation, the more alike the results of the two tests involved. Do this for the correlations between all the tests, and you are then able to pick out the tests giving the highest correlations with all the other tests; they are the ones that best serve to measure intelligence, i.e.the quality all the tests measure with greater or less accuracy. You can of course further analyse the table of correlations to discover groups of specially high correlations defining the tests which measure any of the special abilities mentioned. The methods of statistical analyses are of course highly complex, but the rationale underlying them is as indicated.

Are there other ways of subdividing our tests, and implicitly the aspects of intelligence we are measuring? There is an important difference between two aspects of intelligence already implicit in Cicero's use of the term '*intelligentia*'. The most fundamental definition of intelligence is something like the ability to reason, to solve problems, to learn new material; this is sometimes called *fluid* intelligence because you can shift it easily from one problem to another. But your ability to learn is usually applied to special subjects like geometry, or French, or physics, or geography, or history; you acquire facts and knowledge, and the sum total of what you have thus acquired, at school, or in life may be called *crystallised intelligence*. Of course the two are highly correlated (usually around 0.60 to 0.70), but they are conceptually different. Under ordinary circumstances what you have learned is determined to a large extent by how well you can learn, i.e. crystallised ability is determined by fluid ability, but clearly other factors also play a part. An introverted child likes to read, to study, to learn, while an equally bright but extraverted child likes to play, be with other children, have fun. It is clearly the introvert who is likely to learn more, and do better on tests of crystallised ability. Motivation is important; a child highly motivated to learn will do better than a child not so motivated.

Here are two test items that illustrate the difference between fluid and crystallised ability.

Test of fluid ability: A C F J O   ?

Here every child knows the letters of the sequence, so all children are familiar with the fundamentals of the problem. This is not true of the following problem:

Calliope, Euterpe, Erato, Polyhymnia, Clio,
Melpomene, Thalia, Tepsichore   ?

The answer of course is Urania, the last of the nine Greek Muses, but if you haven't learned about the Muses, you cannot do the test! This would be an example of a *crystallised* test item. Of course, these do not have to be all that difficult; a favourite test of crystallised ability is the vocabulary test, items from which can be quite simple:

	Packet
Haze:	Animal
	Mist
	Haystacks
	Fury

A vocabulary test can be a good test of intelligence because the brighter children (high fluid ability) tend to learn words in the course of their lives (reading newspapers, hearing conversations, listening to TV or radio, talking to parents and teachers, looking at books), whereas duller children with the same or similar experiences, only learn fewer words. Thus no special teaching is required, as it is for knowing the Muses.

Ideally we would prefer tests of fluid intelligence, but most tests use both types of items. Many tests are divided into verbal and non-verbal sections, with the former closer to crystallised ability and the latter to fluid ability. Here is a typical test of non-verbal ability; it is often referred to as a matrices-type test:

Which is the correct figure to complete the matrix?

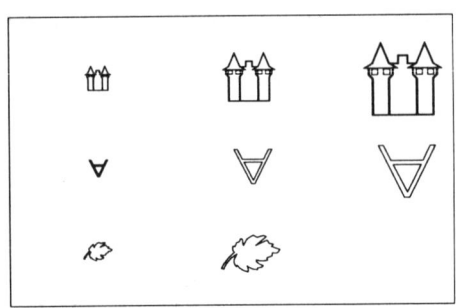

1:  **2:** **3:**

4: **5:** **6:**

One reason for having items measuring crystallised ability is that tests are often used for prediction, and a tendency to work hard is an important part of the prediction of scholastic success; as we have seen, hard work results in better scores in tests of crystallised ability. Another reason is that a short vocabulary test gives very reliable scores, whereas we would need much longer tests of fluid ability to achieve equal reliability. There are many different types of IQ test, depending on the purpose of the test, and the results require skilled interpretation by a trained psychologist to be optimally useful and predictive; different tests may be useful for different purposes. The tests in this book use typical IQ test items, and give a reasonable approximation to your child's IQ, but such do-it-yourself testing cannot and does not substitute for a test carried out by an experienced psychologist, using several different types of test to produce a much more detailed account of your child's pattern of abilities. Always keep this caution in mind!

There is one further division that has been discussed and investigated a great deal over the years, and that relates to the possible opposition between *speed* and *power*. You can construct an IQ test along one of two lines. You can take large numbers of *easy* items, that is items most people will get right, and impose a time limit on the test such that no-one can finish all the items in the time allowed. This way of test construction places a high value on speed; the faster you work, the more problems you succeed in solving. But, many critics objected, this merely discloses a superficial, facile, sort of mind; what is important, is the *power* to solve really difficult items. Thus we have the alternative method of test construction, using test items that are so difficult that only some testees can solve them. Most tests compromise, starting off with easy items, and then going on to more and more difficult ones. But is that reasonable?

The answer seems to be in the affirmative. Children who are *quick* to solve easy items are also good at solving *difficult* items; perhaps *speed of thinking* is the fundamental characteristic of intelligence? It is an inviting idea, and we shall describe some experiments later on to show that there is some truth in it. For the moment, just note that there is no essential opposition between speed and power. They are opposite sides of the same coin. The child who shows the greatest power (can solve the difficult problems) is also the child who works most quickly through a set of easy problems.

Nature and nurture

There have been many battles fought over the question: nature or nurture? People put forward arguments to show that *heredity* (nature) decided what a child's IQ would be, while others argued equally fiercely that it was the *environment* that was responsible — parental influence, school, life experiences and the like. The whole battle, of course, is misconceived totally — without *either* nature or nurture, heredity or environment, we would have no intelligence to argue about. The question is not an either-or one, but a quantitative one — how much is due to heredity, how much to environment? Such quantitative problems demand complex experiments, and equally complex statistics, and only fools would venture an opinion without full knowledge and understanding of all facts and theories involved. We shall briefly list some of the studies that have been done to demonstrate that heredity is important, (but not *all* important), and then go on to discuss the *meaning* of that statement, because this meaning is often completely misunderstood.

The most important fact to realise is that some arguments are completely worthless. If you find that bright parents have bright children, this is often said to prove the importance of heredity. Or it may be used to argue for the importance of environment — bright parents are normally better placed to provide well for their children. Thus either argument is pointless; no proof can be obtained for either side by just looking at what is probably a *combined* effect — bright children inherit their bright parents' genes, and they also are favoured by the good environment bright parents are able to provide. We must look elsewhere for more decisive proof.

Such proof can be found by looking at an experiment performed for us by nature, namely identical (monozygotic or MZ) and fraternal (dizygotic or DZ) twins. Twins can originate because a fertilised egg (ovum) splits in two, thus producing two like-sex individuals having identical heredity — MZ twins. Or two ova may be simultaneously fertilised by two sperms, producing two individuals sharing on average 50% heredity — DZ twins — who may be like-sexed or not, and who share heredity to the same extent as ordinary siblings conceived and born at different times.

We thus arrive at our first demonstration — MZ twins adopted away from their parents at or shortly after birth. The children share identical heredity, but are brought up in quite different environments; will their IQs be similar? The answer is that the correlation between such twins is extremely high — between 0.70 and 0.80! In other words, although brought up in different environments, the twins have IQs that are very similar. We can compute from this that something like 70% of all the observed differences in IQ are due to heredity, 30% to environment. Do other types of investigation support this estimate?

Consider our second demonstration. MZ twins share 100% heredity, DZ twins only 50%; it should follow that, if heredity is important, MZ twins should be more alike in IQ than DZ twins, and indeed that has always been found to be so. We can use the observed difference to calculate the relative contribution of heredity and environment, and low and behold, it turns out to be 70%-30%, very much like our first determination.

Another way of attacking the problem is by looking at ordinary children (not twins) who are adopted at birth, thus growing up in another family. Will their IQ be more like that of their natural parents, or like that of their adoptive parents? The natural, biological parents provided the heredity, the adoptive parents the environment; which is more important? The answer is that adopted children have IQs much closer to that of their true parents than that of their adoptive parents; in other words, heredity is more important than environment. It is an interesting side-light on the problem that as children grow older, their IQs get more and more to resemble those of their true parents! In other words, the longer they are exposed to the environment of their adoptive parents, the less does their IQ resemble that of the adoptive parents who provided that environment. Thus our third demonstration again shows the power of heredity in producing differences in IQ.

Our fourth proof comes from *degree of relationship*. Different degrees of blood relationship (parents and children, uncles, nephews and nieces, cousins, etc) mean different proportions of shared genes, and if heredity is important high consanguinity should mean high similarity in IQ, and low consanguinity low similarity in IQ. Thus parents and offspring correlate 0.50, and siblings reared together 0.45; cousins only correlate 0.14. There is good agreement between consanguinity and similarity in IQ.

Next consider proof number five. Children growing up naturally in our society are subject to all sorts of environmental differences and hazards; under those conditions they show a distribution of IQ like that given in Figure 1. Now imagine a group of children brought up under conditions minimising environmental differences as far as humanly possible; we would expect the distribution to be much narrower, with the children showing a lesser range of IQs — after all, we have abolished most of the environmental factors that could have produced differences! Such conditions have been studied in children's homes, where the children were taken shortly after birth, and where conditions, (feeding, sleeping, schooling, medical care, etc.) were as far as possible identical for all of the children; yet the distribution of IQs was as wide as ever! Similarly in a Polish study, all the children were living under very similar conditions of Communist egalitarianism, with parents earning identical salaries, children going to the same schools, food and medical care being identical as well. Yet differences in IQ were as wide as ever; there were a few very bright and very dull children, more bright and dull ones, and lots of average IQ children. Clearly reducing environmental differences to a minimum had little effect on IQ differences!

Proofs six and seven are opposite sides of the same coin. Most people have heard of 'inbreeding depression', i.e. the tendency of children born of incestuous relationships to suffer more diseases and other problems than children born in normal families. The laws of genetics predict that, if IQ is largely determined by heredity, then children born of incestuous relationships should have *lower* IQs than children born of equally intelligent parents not related to each other. Such inbreeding depression, caused by deleterious genes being more likely to be present in parents themselves related, has indeed been found; the offspring of cousin marriages have lower IQs than expected, and the offspring of father-daughter or brother-sister matings show very low IQ values.

The opposite effect, called heterosis or hybrid vigour, refers to the good effects of pairings with someone from a different race. Where having too similar a gene complement is bad, having a very different gene complement is good; such children show a significantly higher IQ than would usually be expected. Thus inbreeding depression and hybrid vigour, both genetic effects, can be demonstrated for IQ differences.

Our eighth and final proof (there are others, but they are too technical to discuss in detail) relates to a phenomenon that is of considerable social importance, and confounds all those who condemn the postulation of genetic factors because they believe it would lead to a kind of caste system, the children of dull parents forever doomed to a shadowy existence in the lowest caste. The phenomenon was discovered by Galton, and is called *regression to the mean*. What we normally assume when we hear of genetic explanations of IQ differences is that dull parents have dull children, bright parents, bright children, and average parents, average children. But this is only partly true. Consider height. Height is strongly inherited, tall parents do indeed have tall children on average. However, the children tend to be *less tall than the parents*; in other words, they regress to the population mean! Similarly, for very short parents; their children tend to be short, but somewhat taller than their parents! This regression to the mean is predictable in terms of genetic theory; it must occur for any trait, physical or psychological, that is determined to some extent less than 100% by heredity.

Father's status	Son's status					
	1	2	3	4	5	None
High white collar (1)	54	15	12	12	1	6
Lower white collar (2)	45	18	14	15	2	6
Higher manual (3)	28	12	28	24	1	7
Lower manual (4)	21	12	23	36	2	7
Farm worker (5)	17	7	20	29	20	8

Table 2: Mobility of social status — % changes from father to son

That means that IQ, too, should be subject to this law, and the evidence shows without question that IQ regresses to the mean — the children of high IQ parents have high IQs, but lower than their parents, while children of low IQ parents have low IQs, but higher than their parents! This immediately removes the shadow of a caste system from our society; there is considerable generational change in IQ, and this produces considerable social mobility from one generation to another. Table 2 shows the degree of social mobility in our type of society, father's status being compared with son's status, on a five point scale. Where the father is a lower manual worker, of his sons, 21% are in higher white collar jobs, 12% in lower white collar jobs, 23% in higher manual jobs, 36% in lower manual jobs, similar to their fathers. But only one in three is in the same social category as his father, 56% have risen in the social scale, many rise to the top. As a counterweight, of the sons of higher white collar parents, 46% have sunk in the social scale. Thus there is a considerable up and down even in one generation; three generations are sufficient to eliminate most of the social predictability from parents to children.

This up- and down- movement is largely due to differences in IQ. In the same family, the brighter children rise in the social scale, the duller ones go down. To obtain the caste system, we need social planning, like in India; nature does not give us any basis for such an inhuman and detestable grading of human beings for all time, and irrespective of individual merit. A student once tested Brahmins and untouchables in India, and found no difference in IQ!

You may ask why, if each generation shows the extremes contracting towards the middle, do we still have children of very high and very low IQ? The answer is very simple. The great majority of parents (50%) have IQs between 90 and 110; their children sometimes have very high or very low IQs, just making good that deficiency produced by the regression factor. Although, of course, the regression effect is true *on average, some* children of bright parents are brighter than their parents, and *some* children of dull parents, duller than theirs. The segregation of genes, which takes place individually for every child, other than MZ twins, is a cruel lottery which favours some and disfavours others. This is a fact of nature; psychologists and geneticists do not produce the effect, they simply study it.

Often the result is a tragedy for the children of very bright people, who have very high hopes and expectations for their children. Ignorant of the regression effect, they dream of their children being even more successful than they themselves, in school, in college, and in life, only to suffer bitter disappointment when the children are not as bright and successful as the parents had hoped. This often leads to recriminations, blame and withdrawal of love; yet it is not the fault of the child that nature followed its own laws, rather than pay attention to the wishes of parents. We must be realistic, and not punish children for being what they are.

There have been some arguments against the various proofs given for the importance of heredity. Thus, it is said that the environment of the MZ twins adopted at birth have not been all that different. True, but the effect of different amounts of such environmental differences have been found to be minimal. Thus looking at twins being brought up in environments sharing the minimum of similarity correlated 0.70 for IQ, as compared with the total sample of 0.72! Again, it is suggested that MZ twins are treated more alike than DZ twins, and that this may cause the observed differences in correlation. The studies of the special treatment of twins by parents showed no effect on correlations. These are not serious criticisms, and special studies and computations have shown them to be worthless.

The final criticism is that the data on MZ twins brought up separately, published by Sir Cyril Burt, were in part invented. We shall deal with this in a later section, but it may be stated here that the figure of 70% for heredity, 30% for environment was already put forward in 1941 by Professor Woodworth, who had been asked by the American Psychological Association to survey all the available evidence, long before Burt published his data. When the evidence was reviewed in 1979, omitting Burt's data, the same figure of 70% - 30% was arrived at. Burt's data in fact gave identical results to all other studies that have used MZ twins reared apart; whether we use his data or not makes no difference whatsoever.

We have so far discussed the scientific evidence; now allow us to tell you a true story that *illustrates* how these genetic influences actually affect people's lives. A former Cambridge graduate in psychology who had married a head teacher thought that they were unable to have children, and adopted three; both parents were firmly convinced that education was all, and that the talk of genetics was completely irrelevant. But when they moved to Jersey, they found that they were able to have children after all, and proceeded to have another three. They were less able to provide the constant background of help and motivation for their own children because the adopted children took up much of their time, yet the differences in behaviour were startling. The biological offspring excelled at school, carried away all the school prizes, read widely, discussed intellectual, literary and political problems, and never did a stroke of work around the house or the garden. The adopted children never got honours in school, disliked academic learning, preferred active work in the house or the garden, and finally went into blue collar jobs!

Just a story, proving nothing, but sufficient to convince the lady and her husband that heredity is a powerful factor!

What does it all mean?

You may by now be ready to believe that genetic factors are vitally important in determining a child's IQ, but you may not be able to see what exactly that means as far as you are concerned. Does it mean that there is nothing you can do to help your child? Nothing could be further from the truth. If 70% of the differences in IQ between children are due to heredity, 30% are due to environment, and that environment, particularly for younger children, is predominantly provided by parents, then you do have an important part to play. Although 30% may not sound all that much, it does amount to almost one third of the total, and that can make all the difference between success and failure.

But let us be clear about one thing that is often misunderstood. The figure of 70% refers to a particular group of people (British children living at the present time). It is not a *universal* constant, like the speed of light, but is what is known as a *population statistic*, i.e. tied to a particular group. It might be much lower in India, where conditions of wealth and educational advantage are much more extreme than here. Therefore, if in our country environment contributes 30%, then in a country where conditions are much more extreme environment would be expected to contribute much more to the measured IQ. The same would be true of testing in Africa, or any other third world country; *the relative importance of nature and nurture depends on external conditions.*

But this statement goes even further. The 70% - 30% ratio applies to a group, as stated; that also means that it does not apply to individual children! You cannot say that for your son or daughter, the IQ is determined to the extent of 70% by heredity; such a statement is pretty meaningless. Such estimates can be shown to be true and meaningful for groups, but do not apply to individuals. It means that the average amount of environmental influence in a country contributes 30% to individual differences in IQ; that does not mean that for a group of parents making special efforts the figure could not be larger, or for a group of non-caring parents smaller! So do not over interpret the figures given; they definitely show that genetic factors are very important, but environment is also important, and is the only aspect of your child's IQ you can influence.

Let us give you an example of the variability of the hereditarian influence. Scholastic achievement is highly dependent on IQ, and also highly heritable. A study carried out in Norway argued that between 1940 and 1980 the educational system had become much more egalitarian, and therefore the heritability of scholastic achievement should have increased considerably. Studying the records of twins in 1940 and 1980 that is exactly what was found; environment was the more important factor in 1940, heredity in 1980! Thus manipulating the environment can lead to marked changes in the nature-nurture ratio.

But is there any evidence that you can raise the IQ of children by changing their environment? Many efforts to do so have been made, particularly by the American Headstart programme, which introduced a variety of presumably helpful innovations into the school programme for disadvantaged children in the hope that their IQs might be improved, compared to other children not so helped. The outcome of literally hundreds of studies, was not very encouraging; school achievement improved, but IQ only a little, and a year or two after the end of the programme the level of the Headstart children reverted to that of the control. Large scale studies of this kind tend to get lost in bureaucracy, and are not very informative; what happens in small-scale studies?

Several such studies have been published, where considerable efforts were made to help the children, often also involving their mothers, and extending this help into the home. Great successes were often claimed, showing increases in IQ of 30 points or so, but when experts looked into these claims most if not all were discovered to be fraudulent — investigators invented data, or exaggerated effects, or failed to give necessary details. It is interesting that while the alleged successes received widespread acclaim in the media, and special TV shows welcomed the authors, no mention was made of the disclosure of the fraudulent nature of these claims. Thus readers and listeners will still remember the claims, but are ignorant of the disproof! This contrasts vividly with the alleged fraudulence of Burt, suggested but never proved; it was splashed all over the newspapers, received a special dramatic account on TV (Completely false to the actual Sir Cyril in its representation of his life, work and personality), and is often referred to as acknowledged fact when at most the verdict must be 'not proven'.

There is little evidence of the influence of parents, and their ability to improve their children's IQ. Presumably this would extend more to crystallised ability than fluid ability, for obvious reasons, but there is not sufficient evidence to be certain. The evidence is much better as far as schoolwork is concerned; here parental help, enrolment in infant classes and constant encouragement is undoubtedly helpful, as is choice of a good school. Nothing we have said should give the impression that the character of the school is unimportant; all the evidence shows that schools which emphasise strict discipline, hard work, competition and examination results produce much better scholastic achievement than the usual run of schools following the progressive pattern, producing illiterate, innumerate yobs; unemployable and socially useless in spite of what is often a reasonable IQ. A recent government-inspired study in the USA found that nearly half of American adults have such poor literary skills that they are unable to perform tasks any more difficult than filling in a bank deposit slip or locating an intersection on a street map. In other words, they are functionally illiterate!

The Isle of Wight study mentioned earlier did not contain any such inner city schools, run on political-ideological lines emphasising 'modern' or progressive methods — and leading, as in the ILEA-run inner London schools, to some of the worst results in the country, achieved in spite of some of the highest monetary outlay! Even the people responsible for this nonsense have now admitted that they failed the children entrusted to them, a suitable epitaph for theory that inspired mayhem and that paid no attention to fact. As T.H. Huxley once said; 'The great tragedy of science — the slaying of the beautiful hypothesis by an ugly fact!' Careful choice of the school appropriate for the child is the best help parents can give their children. After that (and indeed even before the choice of school becomes important), constant help, advice, cooperation, encouragement of interest in reading and exploring, stress on the importance of education, knowledge, culture — these are all vital to the fostering of whatever the child's IQ may enable the child to understand, learn and comprehend.

It may be useful to end this section by drawing attention to the results of a more refined analysis of the environmentally caused differences in IQ. These may be of two kinds, labelled respectively within-family and between-family, or unshared and shared. Children within one family share many environmental factors, primarily the influence of their parents, the same home environment, probably the same school, the same friends, the same social status. Thus shared influences can be analysed by looking at between-family differences, shorn of any genetic contribution. (We can do this by suitable statistical treatment.) Contrast this with unshared, within-family environmental influences, i.e. different things that can happen to children in the same family. One child may have a good teacher, another a bad one; one may have a bad accident, the other may not; one may hit upon a subject to study which he or she likes, the other may not. There are lots of such accidental differences happening to children in the same family. Which is more important for IQ differences — the shared or the unshared environment?

In his 1941 evaluation of the evidence, already mentioned, Woodworth arrived at an estimate of 20% for shared, between-family environmental effects, as contrasted with 10% for unshared within-family effects. Forty years later, evaluating the very much larger evidence available by then, the same conclusions were reached. It is curious that the many authors who have worked in this area with an environmentalist prejudice never properly addressed the problem of showing precisely what in the environment influenced and affected IQ. Hence we know far more about the genetic contribution than the environmental one — except for knowing that such an environmental contribution exists and is important.

Finally, we may use this section to discuss what has become known as the Pygmalion effect. This alleged effect assumes that teachers, when they know the IQ of a child, will treat that child differently, and thus make the child behave accordingly — an environmental effect that is often alleged to be very strong. It was studied in a well-known experiment where teachers were given imaginary IQs for the children under their care, and it was found that due to the behaviour of the teacher, children's IQs changed to approximate the imaginary IQs they had been assigned. The 'experiment' was riddled with faults of design and analysis, and condemned by every expert reviewer. Furthermore, several psychologists and educators tried to replicate it, and failed; the manipulation had absolutely no effect on the child's IQ! In other words, there is no Pygmalion effect, yet you will often hear it evoked by teachers ignorant of the evidence, but keen to use this alleged 'labelling' effect to discredit IQ testing. There *are* environmental effects on the IQ, but this is not one of them!

The machinery underlying the IQ

So far, so good. We have seen that IQ is *socially important* because it is strongly connected with scholastic success, professional success, high earnings. We have also seen that it is *biologically important*; why else would nature put in place such an elaborate system of inheritance? So obviously the common jibe: 'IQ tests measure nothing but the ability to do IQ tests' is nonsense. As the well-known American psychologist R. J. Herrnstein said:

'It is likely that the mere fact of heritability in IQ is socially and politically important, and the more so the higher the heritability. Because the IQ measures something both heritable and necessary for important social consequences, it cannot be dismissed either as an insignificant biological curiosity or as a wholly arbitrary cultural value. A mere biological curiosity it is not, because of its social predictiveness; a purely cultural artifact it is not, because of its heritability.'

All the same, scientists would like to know a little more about the *nature* of intelligence. All right, we can measure it, but we also want to know what precisely it is that we are measuring. DNA (deoxyribonucleic acid), the principal constituent of chromosomes, is responsible for the genetic contribution to IQ. But all that DNA can do is to produce enzymes and other proteins; it obviously cannot affect behaviour directly. There have to be biological intermediaries — hormonal, physiological, neurological — between DNA and IQ-determined behaviour, and the nature of these intermediaries may give us a clue as to the nature of IQ.

A good beginning here may be Galton's view that *mental speed* may be the fundamental variable involved in IQ differences. He suggested studying such a phenomenon as reaction time in this connection, a suggestion not really taken seriously until quite recently. How do we study reaction time (RT)? Figure 2 shows the console put before the subject. Circles indicate push-buttons, black squares lights that can be flashed on and off. The button in the centre, at the bottom, is the 'home' button. The subject depresses it with his index finger, and waits. When one of the lights flashes on, he moves his finger as quickly as possible to the button in front of the light, and depresses it, thus extinguishing the light. We take two measures. One is of the so-called *decision time* (DT), from the moment the target light comes on to the moment the subject releases the home button. The other is the *movement time* (MT), from the release of the home button to the depression of the target button. RT = DT + MT. The experiment can be of *simple* RT, in which case only one light is involved (always the same), or of *choice* RT, where any one of two, or of four, or of eight lights can be involved. About 100 reactions are measured in order to get a reliable mean value for DT and MT, and we also look at variability, i.e. the degree to which these measures range around the mean. Take two sets of DT measures, taken from Smith and Jones; only ten are given to save space:

Smith: 120 milliseconds, 110, 115, 125, 130, 128, 111, 122, 118, 120.
Jones: 180 milliseconds, 110, 250, 190, 170, 302, 150, 248, 180, 220.

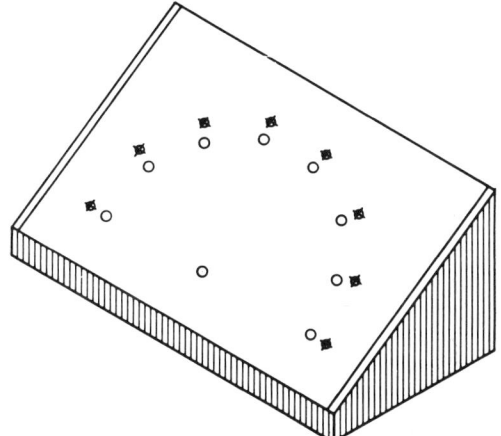

Figure 2: The console used for measuring reaction time
Push buttons are indicated by circles, green jeweled lights by circled crosses. The 'home' button is in the lower centre, six inches from each response button.

The average DT of Smith is 120, of Jones 200 milliseconds, but in addition Smith is much less *variable* than Jones. All his scores are within 10 milliseconds above or below his mean. Jones is sometimes 70 milliseconds below his mean, sometimes 122 milliseconds above. Is there any correlation between RT, or variability, and IQ? The answer is definitely yes. Correlations are low for simple reaction time, and higher for choice reaction time; this is true for DT, but also for MT, although MT is less responsive to changes in the number of lights involved. Most diagnostic are stimulus patterns which pose some slight cognitive problem, like the odd man out paradigm. Here, you present three lights simultaneously, two close together, one some distance apart; the task is to push the button under the light that is some distance from the other two, i.e. the odd man out. Many other variants are possible, and all correlate with IQ; the bright individual reacts more quickly than the dull, although the task is so simple that even mentally retarded children have no difficulties with it.

There is just one problem in claiming that the results bear out Galton's theory. Variability in RT tests correlates even more highly with IQ than simple speed! This is a problem for any theory that states that *mental speed* is fundamental to intelligence. We will come back to this point later.

Another speed test that has been correlated with IQ is the so-called *inspection time* (IT) paradigm. Here we are concerned, not with how quickly a person can react, but with how quickly that person can take in perceptual information. The display consists of two lines of clearly unequal length, joined at the top, like this:

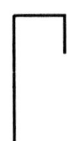

The longer line may be presented on the right or left, and the subject has to press a button in his right or left hand to indicate the correct position. Again the test is ridiculously easy, but the configuration is presented very quickly — from 150 milliseconds down to 20 milliseconds. The question is at what speed of presentation does the subject fail to give the correct answer? This test too correlates well with IQ, the brighter subjects giving correct answers even at very fast presentation. Thus *both* speed of perception and of reaction correlate well with IQ, and combining RT and IT values give us correlations with IQ that are almost as good as those of one IQ test with another! This speaks well for Galton's theory.

He suggested using RT tests because in his time (around 1880) there was no possibility of actually performing experiments directly involving the cortex. Now we have the electroencephalograph (EEG), which records actual brain-waves, and much effort has gone into measuring these and correlating results with IQ measures. In particular, the so-called *average evoked potentials* (AEPs) have been used for good reasons. What is done is to produce a sudden stimulus, usually visual (a bright flash) or auditory (a sudden sound), and look at the waves that result. Look at Figure 3, which shows sets of waves for six bright and six dull children (their IQs are also given). Quite obviously the waves of the bright children are more *complex*, those of the dull children more *simple*; this characteristic correlates quite highly with IQ. Thus here too we find an important biological feature correlating with IQ. How can we interpret this?

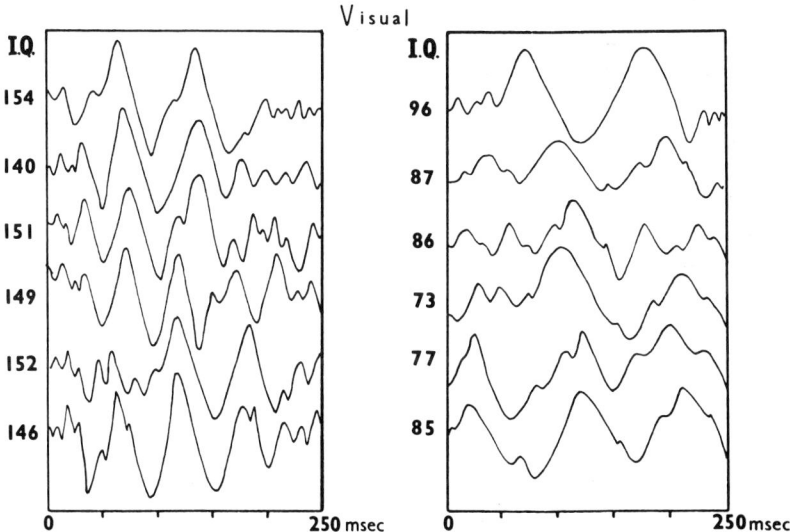

Visual

Figure 3: **Evoked potential waveforms for six high and six low IQ subjects**

Consider how these curves are arrived at. They are the average results of about 100 repetitions of the experiment, each point being the *average* of these repetitions. The reason, as with RT measurement, is to get a good and reliable estimate — there is always some variability around the mean. Now if one person is more *variable* than another, what would happen? Take again Smith and Jones, and give them the AEP test. Look at one particular little configuration, made up of a trough and a peak. Such a configuration can only exist if there is little variability in the sequences of recordings for a given person; troughs must fall on troughs, and peaks on peaks. If a trough falls on a peak, and a peak on a trough, the configuration is eliminated.

	Smith	Jones
	~	~
	~	~
	~	⌣
	~	⌣
	~	~
Average	~	—

For Smith, showing little variability in five measures of his AEP, these add up to a proper trough-peak combination. For Jones, great variability eliminates the configuration. Thus *variability* may be the characteristic feature in the records of the dull children — just as it was in the case of the RT measurements! Only the most outstanding characteristics of the waves resulting from the originating stimulus are retained by the dull, while many relatively minor ups and downs are retained by the bright.

What *causes* variability? The best theory at present available suggests the following.Whenever a stimulus is applied, the afferent ascending pathways carry the message to the cortex; it then passes from neuron to neuron in the cortex, delivering the message to various parts of the brain, until finally a decision is made concerning the appropriate reaction, and the motor cortex is activated. Thus we are dealing throughout with information passing through the cortex. But *errors* may occur in the transmission of information, and when these occur the resulting AEP records will be changed — in other words, *variability* may be a sign of *error proneness*. There is much speculation where in the nervous system these errors may occur; favourite at the moment are the synapses, where the dendrites of one neuron meet the axons of another, and hand over electrically coded information on the dendrite, through chemical transmission in the synapse, to electrical coding in the axon. This complex process can easily go wrong, but there are other places where the integrity of the transmitting mechanism can be impugned.

Do we now have two theories of intelligence — speed and error? Not really. Errors can cause delays in transmission, so slow transmission may only be a manifestation of the presence of errors. The transmission of quite simple information, like: 'The light has gone on', or 'The left line is larger' involves hundreds, if not thousands of neurons, and if errors occur the motor executive has to wait until this has been sorted out. Thus what our DNA determines is a central nervous system and cortex which show different degrees of integrity, allowing few or many errors to occur during the transmission of information, in turn giving rise to many different degrees of speed of information processing. Of course the theory is much more complex than this, but it would not be appropriate to discuss it in any more detail. We only wanted to give you an idea of the kind of theory now being investigated, and the sort of results currently available.

What can IQ testing do to help the child?

There are many ways in which IQ testing has helped children in the past, and can help them in the future. Consider to begin with the *reasons* why IQ tests were introduced originally, and were widely used in selection. In choosing children to go to the better, more academically successful schools, or to university, selection was essentially based on *scholastic* achievement, i.e. the knowledge acquired by the young child. But while this depends to some extent on his or her IQ, schooling makes a great difference — both the standard demanded, and the quality of the teaching. So of course does the ability level of the class — if most have low IQs, the few bright children will not receive a very good education. It follows that working class children are severely handicapped in competing with middle class children; even when equal in IQ, a working class child would usually have been handicapped by receiving an inferior education, thus not likely to be chosen for the better class of higher education.

When Godfrey Thompson in Scotland, and Cyril Burt in England advocated and introduced IQ tests as selection devices; this was done *explicitly* in order to give working class children a better chance by measuring their ability (IQ) rather than their scholastic achievement. In this way the accidental barriers of class were to a large extent removed, and indeed it was shown that many more working class children of high ability were enabled to go on to higher education than prior to the use of

IQ tests. When a Labour Government abolished the 11plus examination, and the use of the IQ test as a selection device, the number of working class children who went on to university dropped markedly. Thus IQ testing has introduced an element of social justice, partly removing the nefarious influence of parental poverty on the future education of bright working class children.

Another benefit the use of the IQ tests can bring is in making possible the making up of classes of fairly uniform ability. Political prejudice has led to the introduction on a wide scale of mixed ability classes, i.e. classes containing children of high, middling and low IQ. It does not need a great deal of common sense to see that such a system makes good teaching impossible, and makes study of school subjects very difficult for most children. The first time the teacher explains something, the bright children understand; the middling ones don't, and the dull ones are bored and don't know what is going on. The next few repetitions by the teacher make the middling bright understand, bores the bright, and leaves the dull still unenlightened. To make even the dull understand, the teacher has to repeat again and again what is amply clear to the bright, and even the middling bright children. It would be difficult to invent a system more likely to reduce the teacher to fury and the children to boredom, often leading to truanting and vandalism, particularly among the dull. No other method guarantees slow progress, maximum friction, and poor results as well as mixed ability teaching does, and the extremely poor results achieved in British and American schools, compared with German, French and Japanese schools are adequate witness to this statement.

Classes selected on the basis of IQ tests produce groups of similar IQ, and have similar ability to learn, making teaching much easier, and learning more pleasant. There are many ways of using IQ tests in this manner, and we will not go into details, but no school should be considered in the forefront of educational advance where routine IQ testing is not in use. Yet we do not even teach budding teachers about IQ testing in our colleges of education, and the few courageous headmasters and mistresses who do introduce it are harassed and criticised.

Quite apart from such general uses of IQ tests, there are more personal ones that can be very important. Consider children who are underachievers. We know roughly how well a child of a given IQ should do; when the child falls below this level, he or she is an underachiever. It is vitally important for parents and teachers to realise what is happening, to try to find out the reasons, and look for remedies. One obvious reason is lack of motivation. A bright child in a mixed-ability class easily gets bored and discouraged, loses interest, and gets up to mischief. He or she may then fall behind, forget about work, play truant or fall into other types of mischief. If you don't know the child's IQ, you may easily think he or she is just not bright enough, and do nothing, when in reality the child is crying out for help — such as transfer to a class of much brighter and higher ability level.

There are many other possible causes for underachieving. We know of an irate parent who brought his son Johnny to the clinic, and said that his school grades were dreadful; what should he do? On testing the child's IQ, it was up in the 140s. What had gone wrong? The child was hard of hearing, and could not follow what the teacher was saying; simply transferring him from the back of the class to the front brought an immediate and spectacular improvement. Uncorrected sight problems can often reveal themselves by causing underachieving, and there are other reasons as well. IQ tests are invaluable in diagnosing the problems; thousands of children could be rescued from undeserved obloquy if only they were tested by an educational psychologist who could diagnose their problem.

Another great advantage of knowing your child's IQ is that you will have some idea of what you can reasonably aim at as far as his or her future is concerned. With an IQ of 120 you can aim at a university education, but with an IQ of 100 that would not be reasonable. Table 1 gives a list of occupations, and typical IQ levels; that may serve as a beginning. Of course your child's preferences, likes and dislikes are also important, as is his or her personality.

These are just some of the advantages of knowing something about your child's IQ. This book will give you a fair idea of where your child is located in the IQ diagram given in Figure 1. But do not take a test given and scored by a lay person too seriously; there are many possible sources of error when you are testing your own offspring.

If you discover a serious problem, you should have the child tested by an experienced educational psychologist who will have available a whole set of tests appropriate to the particular problem in question. Such a psychologist will also be able to deal with many of the problems that often come up in mental testing, such as test anxiety. The IQ you derive from the test here offered gives you a reasonable approximation, but for serious consideration, you want professional advice.

There is one final and pretty obvious use for a book of this kind. Many children and adults nowadays are subjected to selection tests of this kind, and they will be much more likely to do themselves justice if they are familiar with the sorts of problems they are likely to encounter, and have had some experience in trying to solve them. Test sophistication can be very important; it raises your IQ, or your child's IQ by something like 10 points — and in a selection situation, that is well worth having. It may mean all the difference between success and failure!

You may say that practice should not make all that much difference, and that it is unfair if some children have the practice when others do not. Agreed, but then psychologists have always advocated that schools should give children three IQ tests (one each year) *before* the one that acts as a selection device is administered. That would render all children equal — three tests produce the maximum amount of test sophistication the child will find useful. It would also alert the teachers to any sudden catastrophic fall in IQ, due to test anxiety, or sudden illness or some other cause.

But of course educational authorities know nothing about scientific niceties of this kind, so your child's school is not likely to have prepared him or her in this manner. You may find the book's main advantage in providing what a school has failed to provide — your child will be able to give his best when he or she has been properly prepared by actually doing a whole series of tests!

One final remark. We have explained that little can be done to increase the child's IQ — or at least that we have little idea of how to do it — particularly in a type of society where every child goes to school until the age of 16. But there is one way that has been shown to be very effective in raising IQ levels — but only in a minority of children.

To live up to his or her genetic predisposition, a child requires a proper supply of vitamins and minerals, and even apparently well-fed children, preferring junk foods, are often found to be well short of the proper standard. Thuse these children — about one quarter to one third of the population — can benefit from vitamin and mineral supplementation, and have been shown to increase in IQ by more than 10 points! Improvements are greater the younger the child, as one would expect, and are quite long-lasting; if your child is given to a sugary diet, with lots of junk food, it may by useful to try a course of pills to supplement his or her diet. (Of course, this will not benefit children already sufficient in vitamins and minerals.)

It is worth noting that the improvement in IQ was predicted to be in tests of fluid ability, not crystalised ability; if you don't know the names of the nine muses, no dietary supplementation will tell you! But the apparent improvement in the integrity of the nervous system consequent upon such supplementation can and does improve the child's fluid ability; indeed the fact the supplementation works this way is one important proof that the distinction is viable. Note also that there is good evidence to show improvements in scholastic achievement *after* taking the pills: fluid ability increases and enables the child to learn new material better! Supplementation is well worth a try for many children.

Intelligence and communication

In writing (and reading!) about intelligence one is easily led to exaggerate its importance, and underrate other factors that may be even more important for human life. High intelligence is of course essential for solving difficult problems, but probably mainly when these are cognitive, as they are in science and mathematics. People who come up against the IQ literature for the first time often feel that surely here is a way of improving the quality of our political elite, and perhaps of the electorate. Why not select members of the Houses of Parliament, or the Senate and House of Representatives by means of IQ tests? Why not allow only people with high IQs to vote in elections? Such ideas may seem tempting, but they should be disregarded. Political problems are usually indeterminate; there are few known facts, and much guesswork based on intuitive human insight. Logic is not enough, and may lead to outrageous results. What we know of the political judgements of very intelligent and knowledgeable people often sends shivers down one's spine.

As the poet Robert Burns said: 'A man's a man for all that'. Do not ever judge people (including your children!) on the basis of their IQ alone. It is one, and indeed an important one, of the many different facets of human beings, but it is not the only one. Intelligence is relevant to many of the things we do, but so are empathy, altruism, kindness, honesty and many more. For a happy life, and a socially valuable one, those qualities may be much more important than a high IQ. You are more likely to love your children because they are nice human beings than because they have a high IQ; that is a bonus, but it is probably less important than their human qualities. So enjoy your children, but do not hold their low IQ against them, if nature has decided to throw the dice in the segregation of genes that way. High or low IQ — it is not the child's achievement or fault; this is what you and your partner gave the child!

Instructions for giving the test

Instructions for giving the test

Older children can administer the test to themselves, and also score it; for younger children a parent or older sibling should carry out the administration. Tell the child who is the subject of the test that he or she will have *30 minutes* to do the test. Tell the child that it is almost impossible to do *all* the items, so that he or she is not upset by failing to do so. The child should also be told to work quickly, leave items that seem impossible to do after some effort, and to check his or her answers. Guessing is permissible if the child feels that the answer is probably right, but isn't sure. The child should provide paper and pencil to carry out calculations and should have available a list of letters and numbers corresponding to the letters, for help with some problems, like this:

A	B	C	D	E	F	G	H	I	J	K	L	M
1	2	3	4	5	6	7	8	9	10	11	12	13

N	O	P	Q	R	S	T	U	V	W	X	Y	Z
14	15	16	17	18	19	20	21	22	23	24	25	26

Try to persuade the child to regard the whole thing as an exciting game, to reduce his or her anxiety. Do not on any account frighten the child by telling him or her about the importance of the IQ!

Keep exactly to the time limit, don't say 'Oh well, a few minutes to finish this problem won't matter.' They will. Do not answer any questions the child may have about a problem, he or she will have to work it out without your help! What you tell the child afterwards when the IQ has been determined, is your decision, but be sure not to upset the child, or leave him or her in an unhappy frame of mind — even if you have to perjure yourself! Don't let the child do more than one test at a time, it can be exhausting. As stated before, if you have any problems, have the child tested by an educational psychologist, professional advice can be of very great importance! Be sure to let the child work through the set of examples before doing the test proper, so that he or she knows what to expect.

Note: The first four tests are for children aged 10 – 12; the next four for children aged 12 - 15.

Examples

1 Insert missing letter.

A   B   C   D   ___

ANSWER: **E.** ADD 1 TO EACH LETTER.

2 Underline the two phrases that are the closest in meaning.

a) Under no circumstances.

b) Not for love or money.

c) Taken to extremes.

d) Up in arms.

ANSWER: A AND B.

3 Insert the missing word.

20   5   (TEST)   19   20

4   15   (   )   14   5

ANSWER: **DONE.** EACH NUMBER REPRESENTS EACH LETTER POSITION IN THE ALPHABET.

4 Insert the missing word.

B + (paddle) = (pig)

ANSWER: (BOAR). **B + OAR = BOAR.**

5   Insert the word that is a synonym for both of the other two words.

COURAGEOUS   (   )   INDIAN

ANSWER: **BRAVE.**

6   Underline the odd man out from 'examples'.

EXAMPLES: LAMP, AMPLE, SALE, SEXY, MALE, PALES

ANSWER: **SEXY.** THERE IS NO ' Y ' IN EXAMPLES.

7   Insert the missing number.

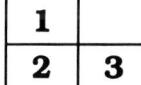 

ANSWER: **6.** RIGHT = TOP LEFT + BOTTOM LEFT.

8   Insert the missing number.

1	2	3	4
2	3	4	5
3	4	5	6
4	5	6	–

ANSWER: **7.** ADD 1 TO PREVIOUS NUMBER.

9   Insert the numbers to make the equation true.

1, 2, 3 and 4

(_ + _) + (_ - _) = 4

ANSWER: (1 + 2) + (4 - 3) = 4

10   Underline whether the final sentence is TRUE or FALSE.

Peter has 15 pence. Paul has 10 pence and Sarah has 20 pence. If Paul gives all of his 10 pence to Peter he will have more money than Sarah.

TRUE   FALSE

ANSWER: TRUE.

11   Using the key, insert the sum of the values surrounding each of the letters.

Key: £ = 3   @ = 4   & = 5

@	£	&	£	&
&	B	@	@	&
@	£	&	£	A
C	&	@	@	£

A: (   )   B: (   )   C: (   )

ANSWER: A = 4 + 5 + 3 + 4 + 3 = 19
             B = 4 + 3 + 5 + 5 + 4 + 4 + 3 + 5 = 33
             C = 4 + 3 + 5 = 12

12   Insert word prefixed by the letters on the left.

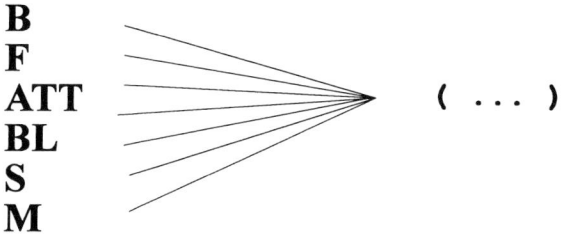

B
F
ATT
BL
S
M

(...)

ANSWER: **END.** THERE ARE ALSO QUESTIONS GIVING SUFFIXES AND FOR A COMMON PREFIX.

13   Insert the number of the missing figure.

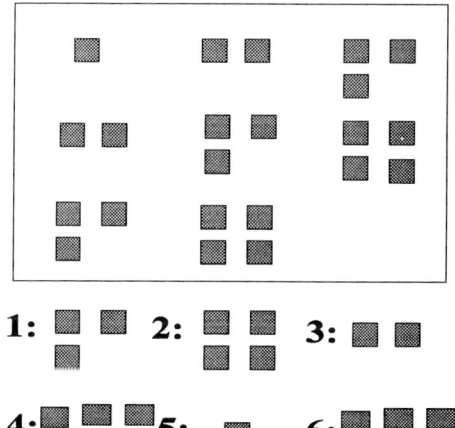

ANSWER: **6.**

14 Insert the missing number.

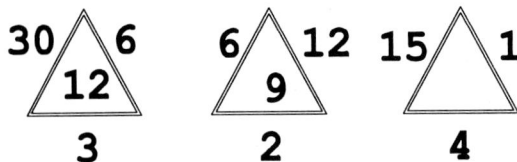

ANSWER: 4. MIDDLE = (LEFT + RIGHT) + BOTTOM.

15 Underline whether the pair of words are SYNONYMS or ANTONYMS.

a) **HIGH** **LOW**
(SYNONYM) (ANTONYM)

ANSWER: **ANTONYM.** ANTONYMS ARE OPPOSITE IN MEANING WHEREAS SYNONYMS ARE THE SAME.

16 Underline the odd man out.

ONE
THREE
EIGHT
HOUSE
TWELVE

ANSWER: **HOUSE.** THE OTHERS ARE NUMBERS.

17 Insert the missing number.

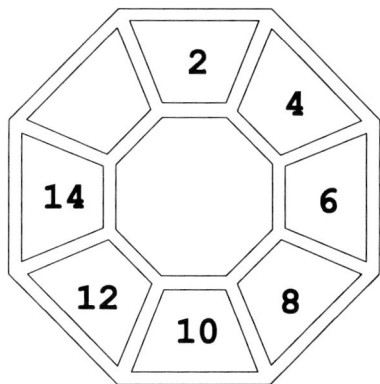

ANSWER: **16.** ADD **2** TO PREVIOUS NUMBER. THERE ARE SIMILAR QUESTIONS USING LETTERS.

18 Insert the missing number.

1 2 3 4 ___

ANSWER: **5.** ADD **1** TO PREVIOUS NUMBER.

19 What is this anagram?

DLOG   (_____)

ANSWER: **GOLD.**

20 Insert the word that completes the first word and starts the second.

DOOR (___) POWER

ANSWER: **MAN.** (DOORMAN AND MANPOWER).

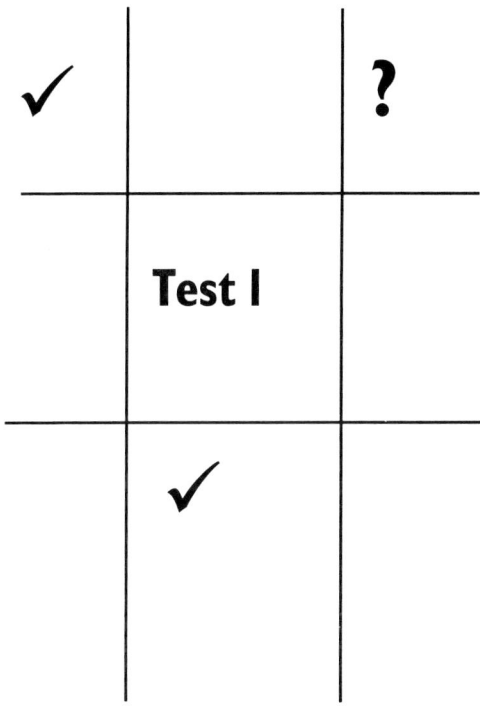

1   Insert the number of the missing figure.

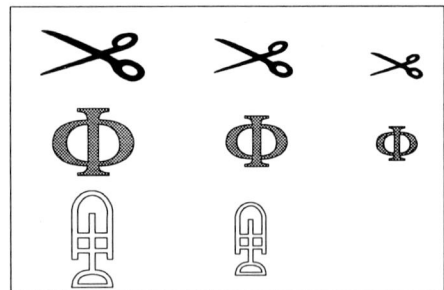

1: Φ   2: ✂   3: [figure]

4: ✂ 5: [figure]   6: Φ

2   Insert the missing word.

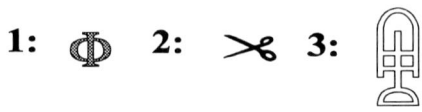

2   1   (BACK)   3   11

5   1   (   )   3   8

3   Insert the missing number.

35   31   27   23   19   (   )

4   What is this anagram?

SEMUO   (   )

5　Insert the missing number.

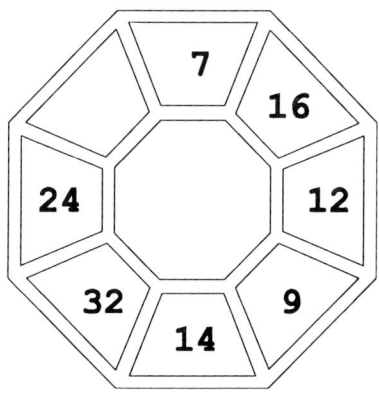

6　Insert the missing letter.

E　　I　　M　　Q　　(　　)

7　Insert the number of the missing figure.

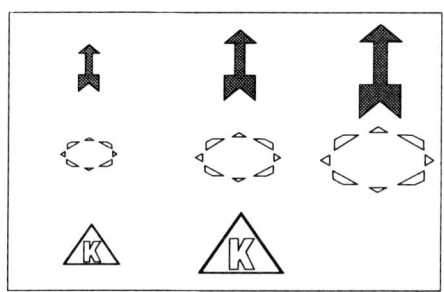

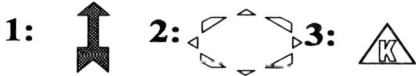

8   Insert the numbers to make the equation true.

3, 4, 5 and 6

(_ x _) - (_ + _) = 11

9   Underline the two phrases closest in meaning.

a) Wash the dishes.

b) Take a break.

c) Take the strain.

d) Have a holiday.

10   Insert the missing number.

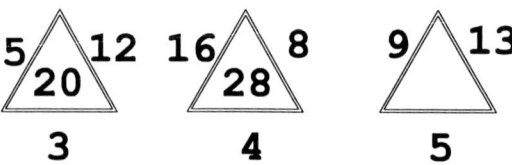

11   Underline the odd man out.

DRUM

TREE

PIANO

GUITAR

VIOLIN

12   Insert the missing number.

6   15   24   33   42   (   )

13   Insert the missing letter.

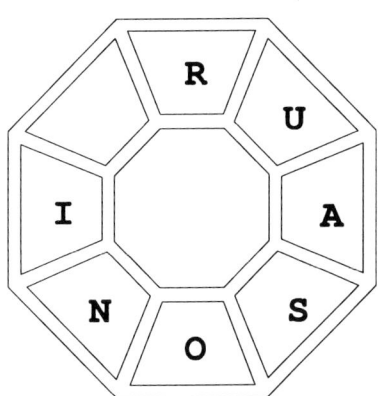

14   What is this anagram?

HLOSOC   (   )

15   Insert the missing letters.

B   F   (   )   N   R   (   )

16   Insert the number of the missing figure.

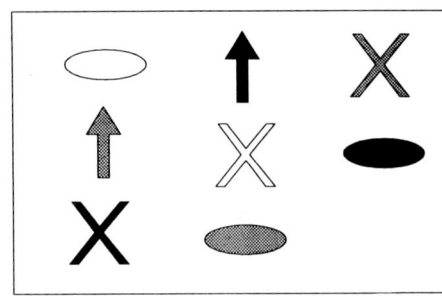

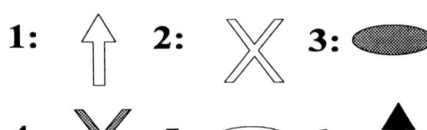

17   Insert the missing number.

7	12	5
14	6	4
10	8	( )

18   Underline whether the final sentence is TRUE or FALSE.

Peter has 3 apples, 2 melons and 5 oranges. He eats 3 oranges and 2 apples. Peter now has more apples than oranges.

TRUE   FALSE

19 Underline whether each pair of words are SYNONYMS or ANTONYMS.

a) **TRIUMPH**   **SUCCESS**

(SYNONYM)   (ANTONYM)

b) **GIANT**   **DWARF**

(SYNONYM)   (ANTONYM)

c) **LEVEL**   **EVEN**

(SYNONYM)   (ANTONYM)

20 Insert the missing number.

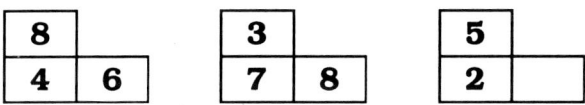

8	
4	6

3	
7	8

5	
2	

21 Insert the number of the missing figure.

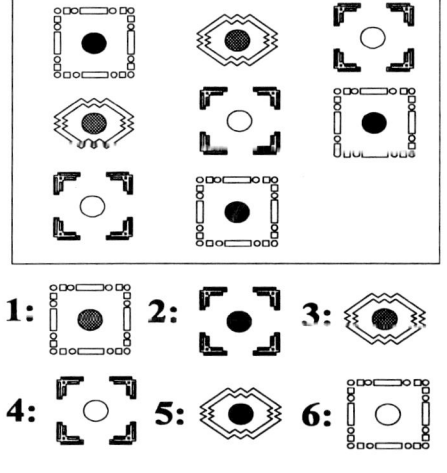

22 Insert the missing word.

19   20   (STOP)   15   16

11   9   (   )   20   5

23 Insert the missing number.

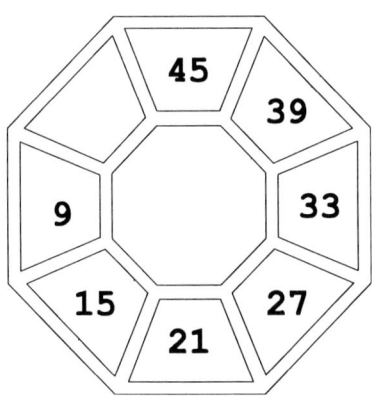

24 Using the key, insert the sum of the values surrounding each of the letters.

Key: % = 4   # = 6   + = 7

+	#	%	%	+
P	%	+	+	#
#	+	Q	+	#
%	%	#	%	R

P: (   )   Q: (   )   R: (   )

25   What is this anagram?

RONOTAC   (   )

26   Insert the missing numbers.

1   (   )   9   27   (   )   243

27   Underline the two phrases closest in meaning.

a) Change one's mind.

b) Bridge the gap.

c) Make a u-turn.

d) Grin and bear it.

28   Insert the missing number.

4 △ 6   5 △ 3   8 △ 3
  18   38
  3   7   4

29   Insert the missing letters.

W   T   (   )   N   K   (   )

30   Insert the number of the missing figure.

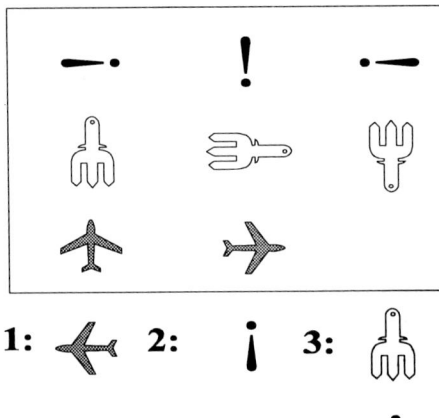

1: 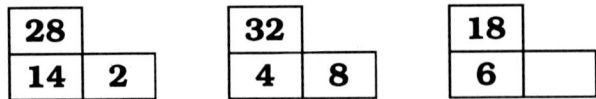 **2:** **3:** **4:** **5:** **6:**

31   Insert the missing number.

28	
14	2

32	
4	8

18	
6	

32   Underline whether the final sentence is TRUE or FALSE.

George takes 10 minutes to get to school. Paul takes 20 minutes and Sarah takes 30 minutes. If Sarah leaves home 15 minutes before Paul she will arrive at school before him.

TRUE   FALSE

33   Insert the missing letter.

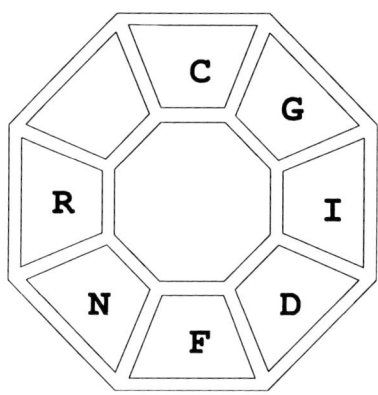

34   Using the key, insert the sum of the values surrounding each of the letters.

Key: $ = 5   £ = 6   & = 9

$	$	£	$	A
£	L	&	£	&
£	&	$	&	$
&	$	T	&	£

A: (   )   L: (   )   T: (   )

35   Insert the numbers to make the equation true.

3, 5, 8 and 9

(_ + _) x (_ - _) = 8

36 Underline the odd man out.

BROADWAY

MAYFAIR

VINE STREET

PALL MALL

TRAFALGAR SQUARE

37 What is this anagram?

OYNMEK   (   )

38 Insert the number of the missing figure.

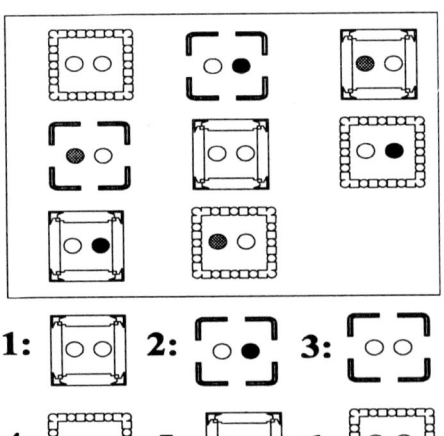

39   Insert the missing numbers.

   58   (   )   40   31   (   )   13

40   Underline whether each pair of words are SYNONYMS or ANTONYMS.

   a) **INTREPID**   **FEARLESS**

   (SYNONYM)   (ANTONYM)

   b) **REVELRY**   **CELEBRATION**

   (SYNONYM)   (ANTONYM)

   c) **FRAILTY**   **STRENGTH**

   (SYNONYM)   (ANTONYM)

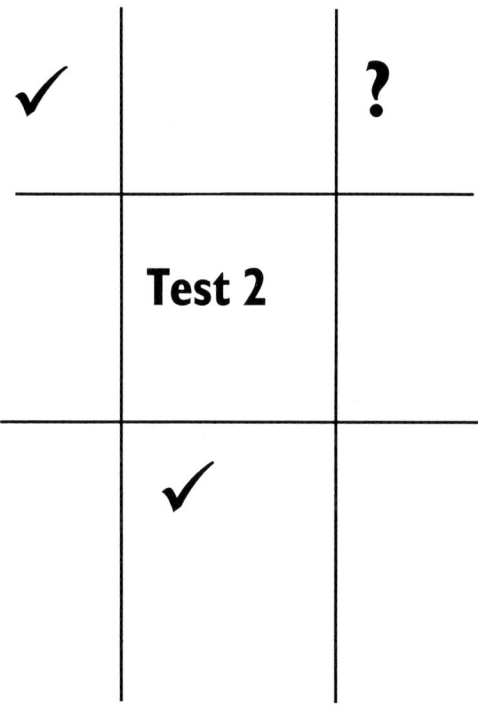

1 Insert the number of the missing figure.

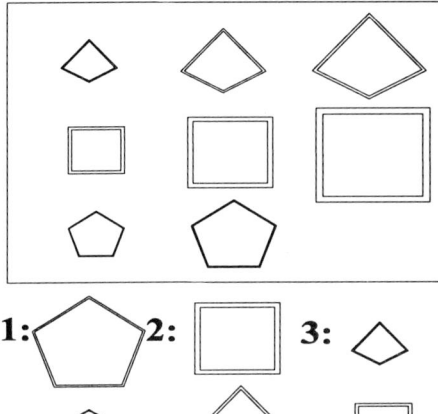

1: **2:** **3:** **4:** **5:** **6:**

2 Insert the numbers to make the equation true.

2, 3, 7 and 8

(_ + _) x (_ - _) = 45

3 Insert the missing number.

8   15   22   29   36   (   )

4 Underline whether each pair of words are SYNONYMS or ANTONYMS.

a) **HURRY** **WADDLE**

(SYNONYM) (ANTONYM)

b) **FEAR** **DREAD**

(SYNONYM) (ANTONYM)

c) **CONTINUE** **WAIT**

(SYNONYM) (ANTONYM)

5 Underline the two phrases closest in meaning.

a) The show must go on.

b) On reflection.

c) Carry the can.

d) In hindsight.

6 What is this anagram?

RVEIR (   )

7   Insert the missing number.

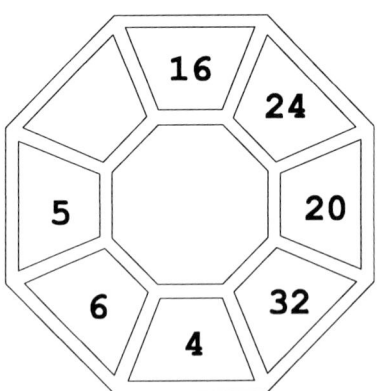

8   Insert the missing letter.

X   U   R   O   (   )

9   What is this anagram?

ROACRT   (   )

10   Insert the number of the missing figure.

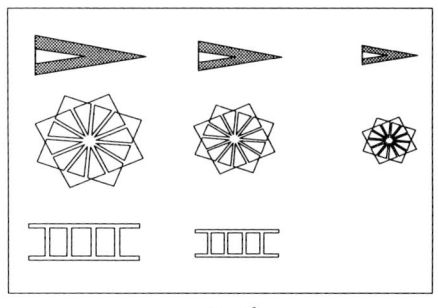

11   Insert the missing number.

```
 9     6    20
12    10    13
17    22    ( )
```

12   Underline whether the final sentence is TRUE or FALSE.

Sue has 10 videos each lasting 90 minutes. If she watches 60 minutes each day, in less than 20 days she will have seen them all.

        TRUE   FALSE

13 Underline the odd man out.

EAST

WEST

SOUTH

NORTH

DIAGONAL

14 Insert the missing number.

15 Insert the missing word.

3   1   (CAKE)   11   5

4   5   (   )   1   12

16   Insert the number of the missing figure.

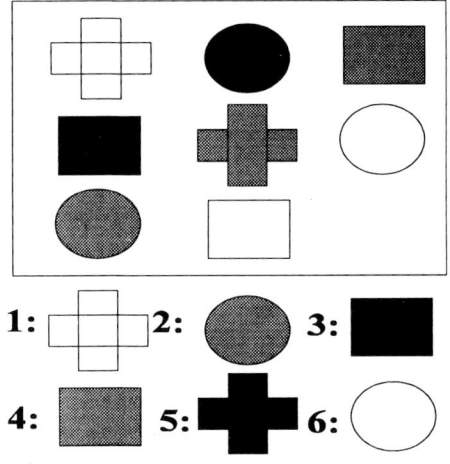

1:    2:   3:

4:    5:   6:

17   Insert the missing number.

47   41   35   29   23   (   )

18   Insert the missing letter.

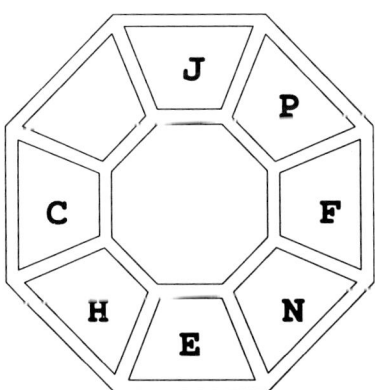

19 Insert the missing number.

6	
9	8

7	
6	10

18	
2	

20 Using the key, insert the sum of the values surrounding each of the letters.

Key: % = 3 $ = 6   ! = 9

$	R	%	!	%
%	$	%	Z	!
$	!	!	$	$
C	%	!	$	!

C: (   )   R: (   )   Z: (   )

21 Insert the missing number.

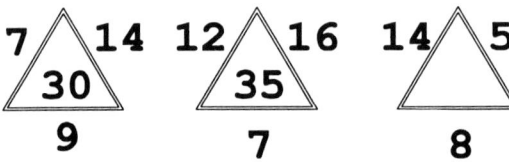

22 Insert the missing word.

8   21   (HUNT)   14   20

23   1   (   )   19   16

23 Insert the missing numbers.

128   64   (   )   16   (   )   4

24 Insert the number of the missing figure.

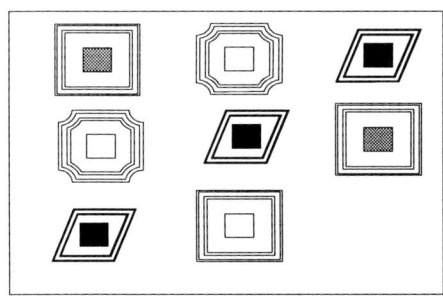

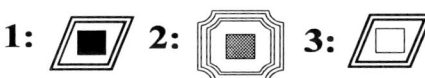

25 What is this anagram?

ILPCEN   (   )

26   Insert the missing number.

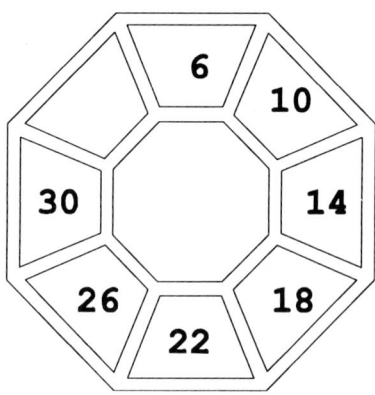

27   Underline whether the final sentence is TRUE or FALSE.

Louise is 4 feet tall, Anne is 4 feet 2 inches tall and Tony is 4 feet 4 inches tall. Louise grows 5 inches, Anne grows 2 inches and Tony grows 2 inches. Louise is now taller than Tony.

TRUE   FALSE

28 Insert the number of the missing figure.

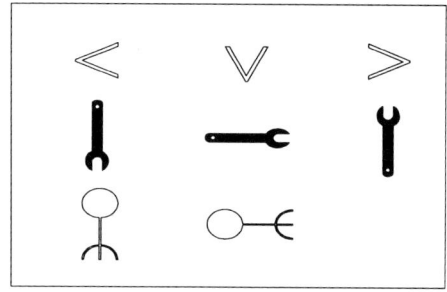

1:  2: Y̧ 3: <

4: ⊱◯ 5: ∧ 6: ꜱ▬

29 Insert the missing number.

18	
13	31

23	
16	39

37	
14	

30 Underline whether each pair of words are SYNONYMS or ANTONYMS.

a) **BROADEN**   **DECREASE**

(SYNONYM)   (ANTONYM)

b) **VAGUE**   **DEFINITE**

(SYNONYM)   (ANTONYM)

c) **HYSTERIA**   **FRENZY**

(SYNONYM)   (ANTONYM)

31 Underline the odd man out.

CLOWN

ASTRONAUT

JUGGLER

FIRE-EATER

TIGHTROPE WALKER

32 Insert the missing letters.

K   M   O   (   )   S   (   )

33 Insert the missing letter.

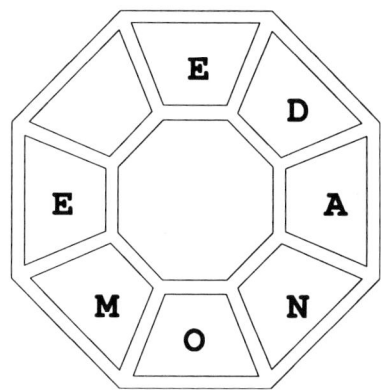

34 Insert the missing numbers.

62   55   48   (   )   34   (   )

35 What is this anagram?

ARGOND   (   )

36 Insert the missing number.

3, 5, 8 and 9

(__ x __) + (__ - __) = 16

37   Using the key, insert the sum of the values surrounding each of the letters.

Key: £ = 5   ! = 7   & = 9

£	&	&	!	A
&	!	!	&	£
E	£	!	C	£
!	!	£	&	!

A: (   )   C: (   )   E: (   )

38   Underline the two phrases closest in meaning.

a) Plough on.

b) Carry on regardless.

c) Brush one's hair.

d) Lose one's footing.

39   Insert the missing letters.

Z   U   (   )   K   F   (   )

40 Insert the number of the missing figure.

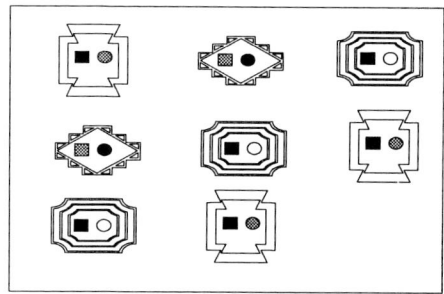

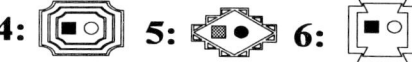

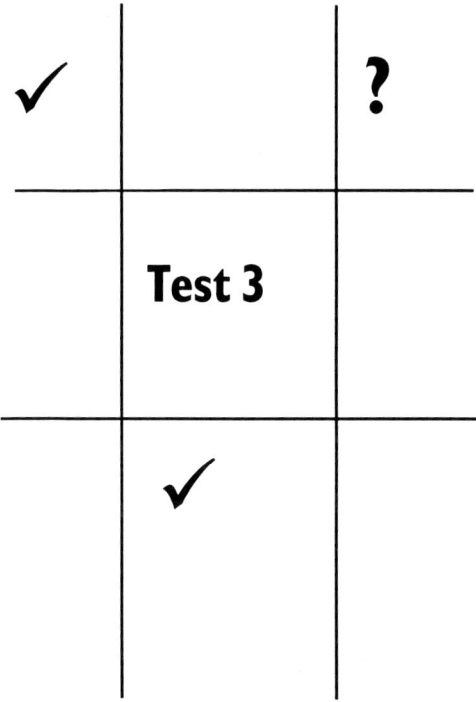

1 Insert the number of the missing figure.

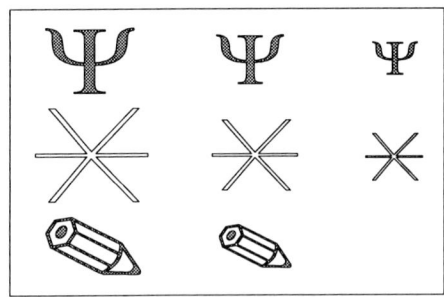

1: Ψ   2: ✳   3: ✏

4: ✳   5: ✏   6: Ψ

2 Insert the missing number.

16	18	5
12	3	12
4	11	( )

3 Insert the missing number.

9   17   25   33   41   ( )

4 What is this anagram?

KCOLC   (   )

5 Underline the odd man out.

MONDAY

FRIDAY

THURSDAY

BIRTHDAY

WEDNESDAY

6 Insert the missing word.

13   9   (MINT)   14   20

6   1   (   )   3   5

7 Insert the missing letter.

C   H   M   R   (   )

8 Insert the number of the missing figure.

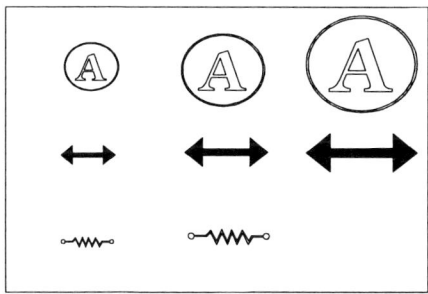

9   Insert the missing number.

17	
8	6

4	
22	5

12	
13	

10   Insert the missing letter.

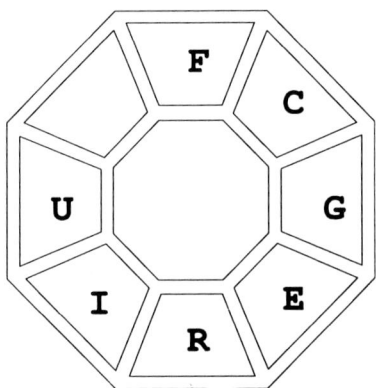

11   Underline whether the final sentence is TRUE or FALSE.

Stephanie buys 2 weekly comics, 3 monthly comics and a rack which holds 20 comics. After 2 months she will still have spaces left on the rack.

            TRUE   FALSE

12   Insert the missing number.

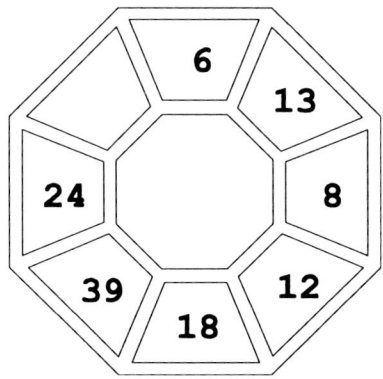

13   Underline the two phrases closest in meaning.

a) Once and for all.

b) In black and white.

c) In the nick of time.

d) Before it's too late.

14   Insert the missing number.

52   49   46   43   40   (   )

15 Using the key, insert the sum of the values surrounding each of the letters.

Key: @ = 4 £ = 5 ! = 7

!	£	£	!	£
M	@	£	V	!
!	@	@	£	@
£	!	!	!	P

M: (   ) P: (   ) V: (   )

16 What is this anagram?

DRCEOR   (   )

17 Insert the missing number.

  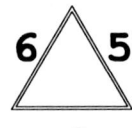

18 Insert the number of the missing figure.

19 What is this anagram?

TPSERO   (   )

20 Underline whether each pair of words are SYNONYMS or ANTONYMS.

a) **EXCITING**   **BORING**

(SYNONYM)   (ANTONYM)

b) **LIKE**   **ENJOY**

(SYNONYM)   (ANTONYM)

c) **CLUE**   **HINT**

(SYNONYM)   (ANTONYM)

21 Insert the numbers to make the equation true.

2, 5, 7 and 8

(_ - _) + (_ x _) = 17

22 Underline the two phrases closest in meaning.

a) Play your cards right.

b) Dice with death.

c) Take one's life in one's hands.

d) Fly off the handle.

23 Insert the number of the missing figure.

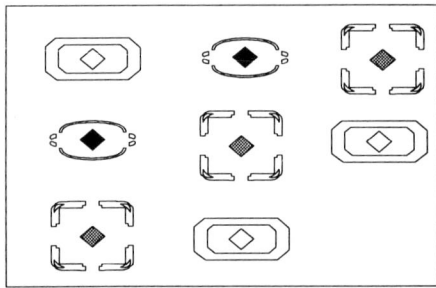

24   Insert the missing number.

4	
5	20

2	
9	18

7	
6	

25   Underline whether the final sentence is TRUE or FALSE.

Julia has a set of books to read. The set comprises 5 books each with 200 pages. If she reads 130 pages a day, she will finish the set in 7 days.

TRUE   FALSE

26   Insert the missing number.

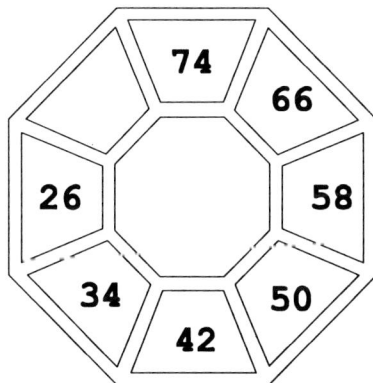

27 Underline the odd man out.

PEACH

ORANGE

VANILLA

BANANA

PINEAPPLE

28 Insert the missing word.

4   9   (DICE)   3   5

12   5   (   )   6   20

29 Insert the missing numbers.

2   4   8   ( )   32   ( )

30 Insert the missing letters.

F   I   L   ( )   R   ( )

31 What is this anagram?

HLGTIF   (   )

32 Insert the number of the missing figure.

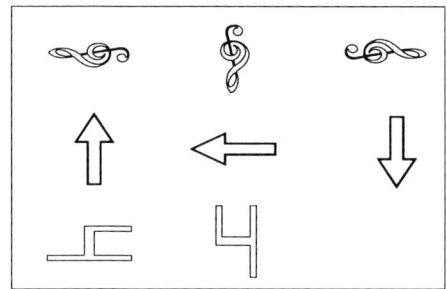

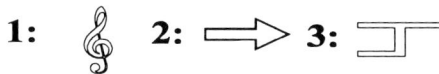

33 Insert the numbers to make the equation true.

3, 4, 5 and 6

(__ - __) + (__ x __) = 13

34 Insert the missing number.

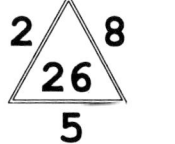 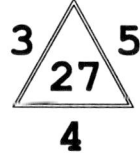 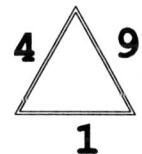

35 Insert the missing letters.

P   N   L   (   )   H   (   )

36   Insert the missing letter.

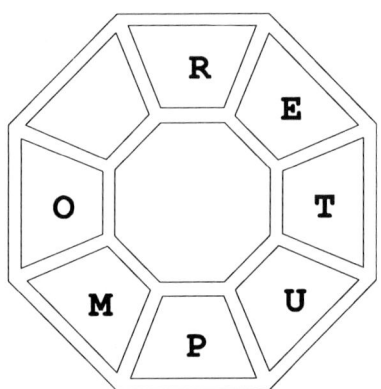

37   Using the key, insert the sum of the values surrounding each of the letters.

<u>Key:</u>   @ = 3   ! = 8   + = 9

X	+	+	@	!
!	@	!	!	!
!	U	+	@	K
+	@	@	!	+

K: (   )   U: (   )   X: (   )

38 Underline whether each pair of words are SYNONYMS or ANTONYMS.

   a) **PUNCTUAL**   **PROMPT**

   (SYNONYM)   (ANTONYM)

   b) **ILLUMINATED**   **DARK**

   (SYNONYM)   (ANTONYM)

   c) **VIVID**   **UNCLEAR**

   (SYNONYM)   (ANTONYM)

39 Insert the missing numbers.

   5   17   (   )   41   53   (   )

40 Insert the number of the missing figure.

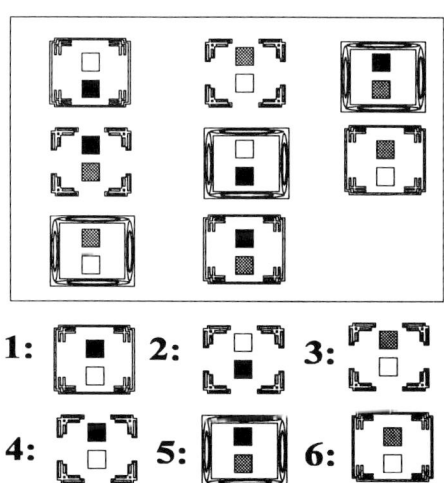

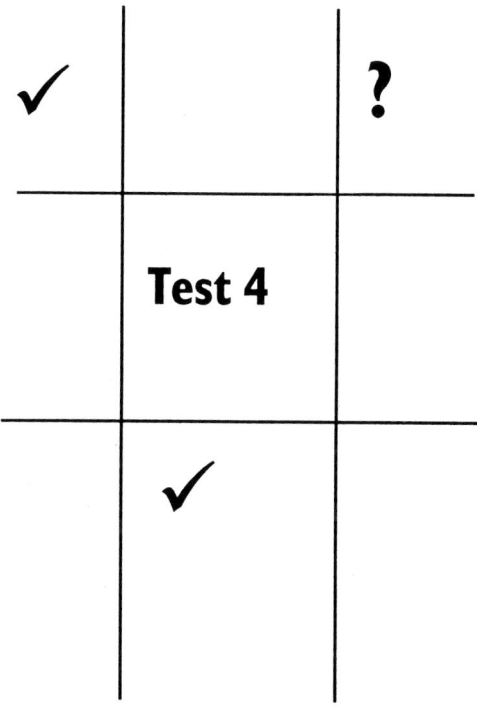

1   Insert the number of the missing figure.

2   Insert the missing word.

1   18   (ARCH)   3   8

7   18   (   )   9   16

3   Insert the missing number.

16   22   28   34   40   ( )

4   What is this anagram?

NILFA   (   )

5   Insert the missing number.

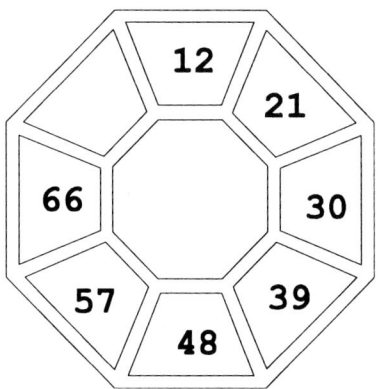

6   Insert the missing letter.

T   P   L   H   (   )

7   Underline the odd man out.

SHOE

CLOG

SLIPPER

BOOT

GLOVE

8   Insert the missing number.

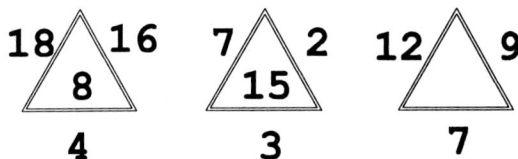

9   Underline the two phrases closest in meaning.

a) Good as gold.

b) Stick to one's task.

c) On the right track.

d) Well behaved.

10   Insert the number of the missing figure.

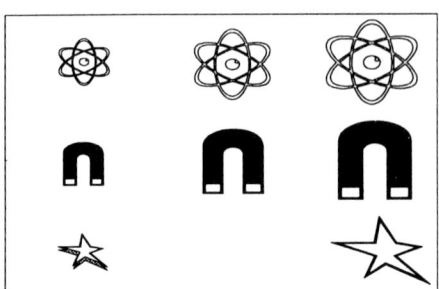

11 Insert the missing number.

14	
3	11

21	
5	2

8	
7	

12 Underline whether the final sentence is TRUE or FALSE.

Fred can walk to the shops in 20 minutes and Colin can run it in 5 minutes. If Fred starts 10 minutes before Colin then he will arrive at the shops before him.

TRUE   FALSE

13 Insert the missing number.

53   45   37   29   21   (   )

14 Underline whether each pair of words are SYNONYMS or ANTONYMS.

a) **EVIDENT**   **CLEAR**

(SYNONYM)   (ANTONYM)

b) **PERFECT**   **FLAWED**

(SYNONYM)   (ANTONYM)

c) **BLAME**   **CRITICIZE**

(SYNONYM)   (ANTONYM)

15   Insert the numbers to make the equation true.

3, 5, 6 and 8

(__ + __) x (__ - __) = 27.

16   What is this anagram?

CRAUSE   (   )

17   Insert the missing letter.

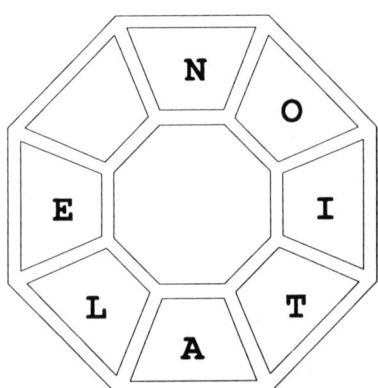

18 Insert the number of the missing figure.

19 Insert the missing number.

14	3	10
6	8	13
20	5	( )

20 Using the key, insert the sum of the values surrounding each of the letters.

<u>Key:</u> # = 3   & = 6   £ = 9

&	L	#	&	#
#	£	#	&	£
£	#	£	K	&
M	&	£	&	#

K: (   )   L: (   )   M: (   )

21 Insert the missing letters.

B   E   (   )   K   N   (   )

22 Underline the odd man out.

TEA

CHEESE

COFFEE

MILK

WINE

23 What is this anagram?

TAERKC   (   )

24 Insert the number of the missing figure.

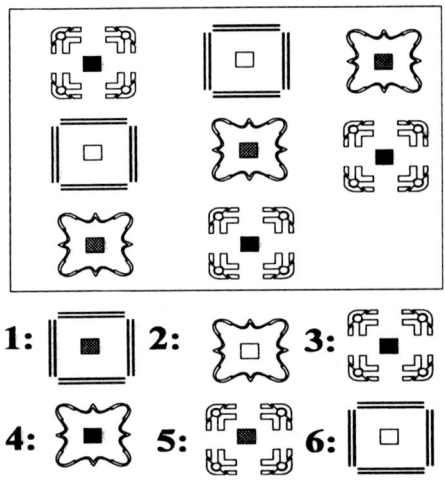

25 Insert the missing number.

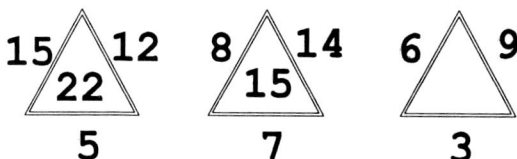

15 ∕\ 12   8 ∕\ 14   6 ∕\ 9
  \22/   \15/   \ /
   5   7   3

26 Underline whether the final sentence is TRUE or FALSE.

Debbie has 5 pairs of shoes, Pam has 6 pairs and Mary has 8 pairs. If Mary gives Debbie 2 pairs of shoes then Debbie will have the most pairs of shoes.

TRUE   FALSE

27 Using the key, insert the sum of the values surrounding each of the letters.

Key: % = 5   ! = 7   @ = 8

C	!	%	!	%
%	@	!	A	%
!	%	@	!	@
@	!	B	@	!

A: (   )   B: (   )   C: (   )

28 Insert the missing numbers.

243   81   (   )   9   (   )   1

29   Underline whether each pair of words are SYNONYMS or ANTONYMS.

a) **NEUTRAL**   **BIASED**

(SYNONYM)   (ANTONYM)

b) **TORRENT**   **FLOOD**

(SYNONYM)   (ANTONYM)

c) **REGULAR**   **SPORADIC**

(SYNONYM)   (ANTONYM)

30   Insert the numbers to make the equation true.

2, 7, 8 and 9

(_ x _) + (_ - _) = 18.

31   Insert the missing word.

26   15   (ZONE)   14   5

23   9   (   )   19   5

32   What is this anagram?

OYLEWL   (   )

33 Insert the number of the missing figure.

34 Insert the missing letter.

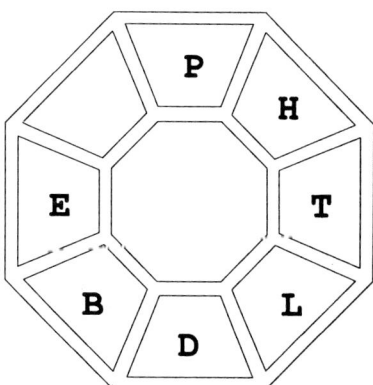

35   Underline the two phrases closest in meaning.

      a) Turn out for the best.

      b) Throw in the towel.

      c) Scare the living daylights out of.

      d) Give up the ghost.

36   Insert the number of the missing figure.

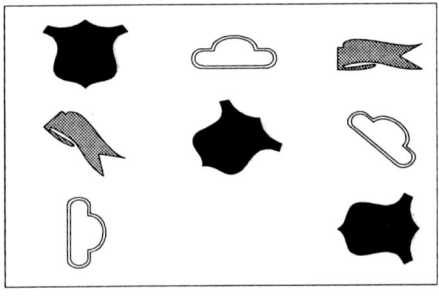

    1:   **2:**   **3:**

    4:   **5:**   **6:**

37   Insert the missing number.

15	
8	7

25	
16	9

32	
11	

38 Insert the missing letters.

Z   U   P   (   )   F   (   )

39 Insert the missing number.

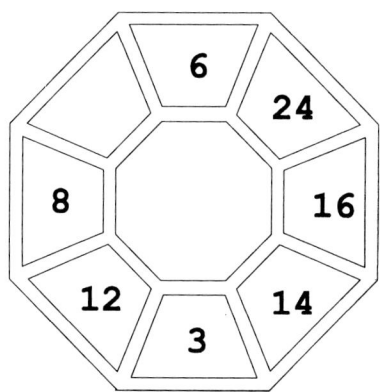

40 Insert the missing numbers.

4   (   )   30   (   )   56   69

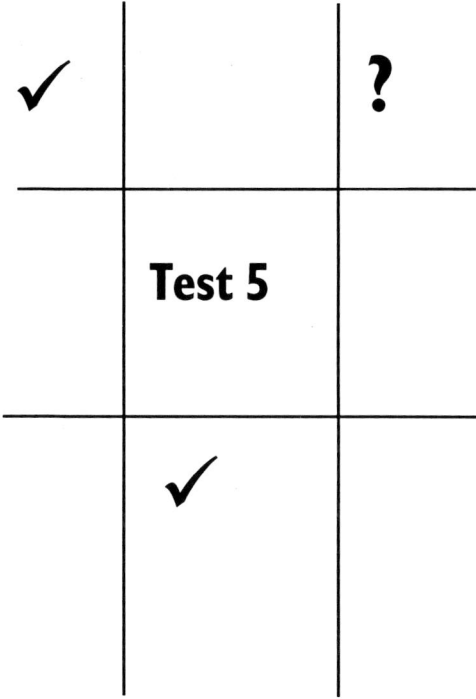

1   Insert the number of the missing figure.

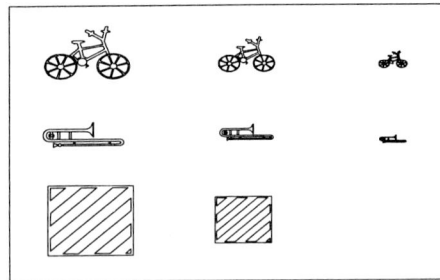

1:   **2:**   **3:**

4:   **5:**   **6:**

2   Insert the missing number.

       6   12   __   24   30   36

3   What is this anagram?

       RENTVAILS   (_____)

4   Underline the odd man out.

CAIRO

ROME

MADRID

GOTHENBURG

COPENHAGEN

5   Insert the missing number.

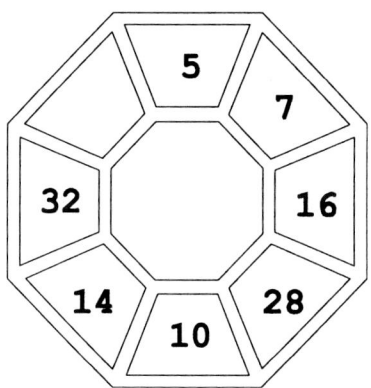

6   Insert word prefixed by the letters on the left.

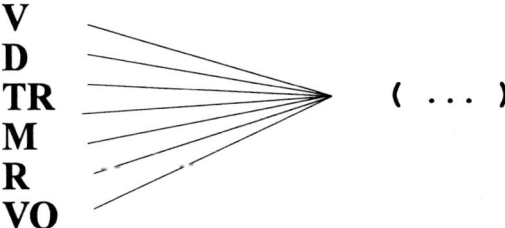

V
D
TR
M
R
VO

(...)

7   Insert the missing letter.

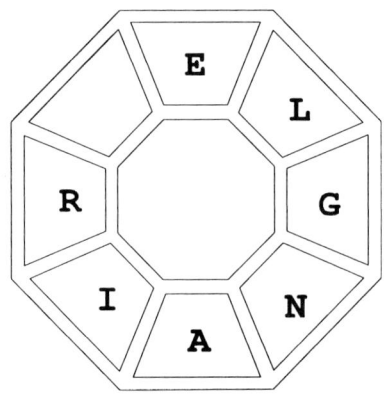

8   Insert the missing numbers.

17   __   51   68   85   __

9   Insert the number of the missing figure.

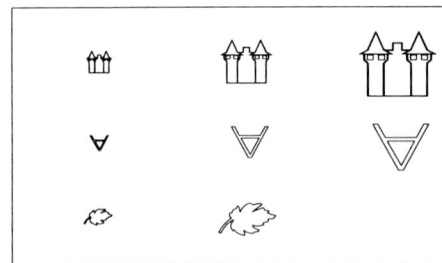

1: ⋁ **2:** 🍂 **3:** 🏰

4: 🏰 **5:** ⋁ **6:** 🍁

10 Insert the word that completes the first word and starts the second.

WHITE (____) BASIN

11 Insert missing letter.

C   G   K   _   S   W

12 Insert word suffixed by the letters on the right.

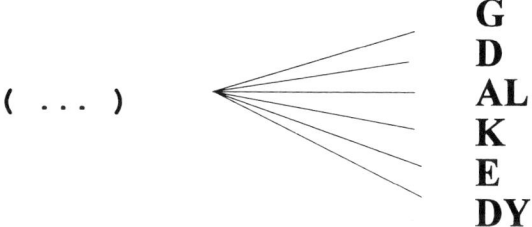

(...)

G
D
AL
K
E
DY

13 Underline the two phrases that are the closest in meaning:

a)   Blown up out of all proportion.

b)   Taken out of context.

c)   A storm in a teacup.

d)   A watched kettle never boils.

14 Insert the missing letter.

Q   N   R   O   S   _

15 Insert the missing word.

5   22   (COVE)   15   3

5   26   (   )   1   13

16 Insert the missing number.

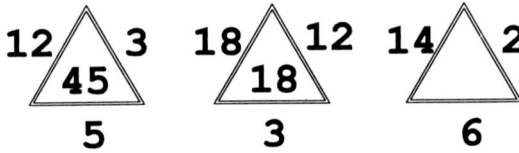

17 Insert the missing word.

B + (endanger) = (quick)

(   )

18 Insert the word that is a synonym for both of the other two words.

MAY (   ) POWER

19 Insert the number of the missing figure.

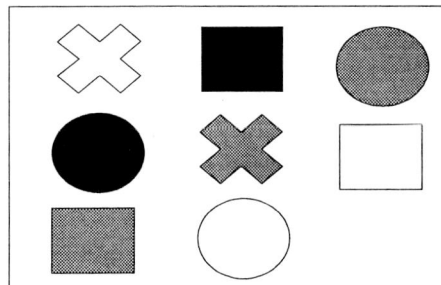

20 What is this anagram?

DICESEXER   (_____)

21 Underline the odd man out from 'elaborate'.

ELABORATE: BEER, REBEL, TARE, TRAIL, REAL, TABLE

22 Insert the missing number.

4	12	16	20
6	10	24	12
8	18	12	14
5	11	19	

23   Insert the missing word.

CON +   (channel)   =   (behaviour)

(   )

24   Insert the numbers to make the equation true.

4, 6, 7 and 8

(_ + _) x (_ - _) = 22

25   Insert the number of the missing figure.

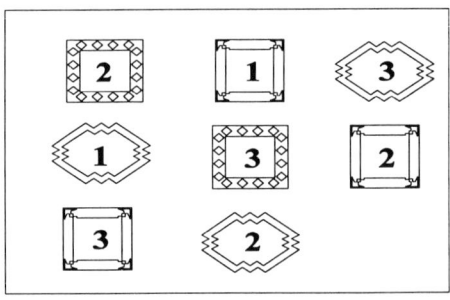

26 Insert the word that is a synonym for both of the other two words.

FRAGMENT (   ) FIGHT

27 Insert the missing number.

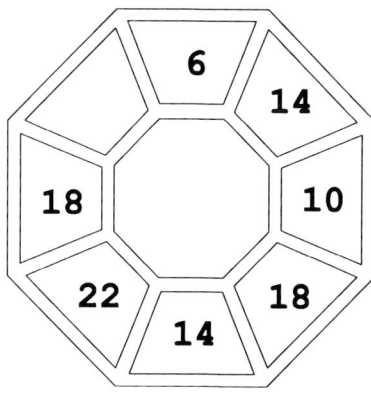

28 Underline the odd man out.

JADE

RUBY

CARMINE

CRIMSON

SCARLET

29 Underline whether the final sentence is TRUE or FALSE.

All muffins are battleships. All battleships have green hair but are bad chess players. Only good chess players can speak French. Therefore all muffins can speak French.

TRUE   FALSE

30 Insert the missing letter.

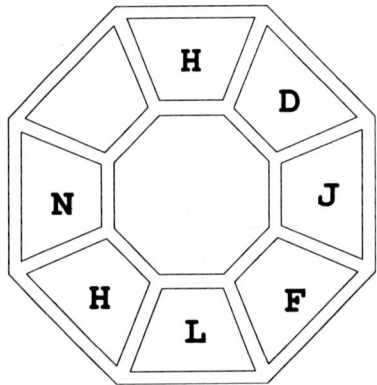

31 Underline whether each pair of words are SYNONYMS or ANTONYMS.

a) **GRADUATION**   **REGRESSION**

(SYNONYM)   (ANTONYM)

b) **RANCID**   **SOUR**

(SYNONYM)   (ANTONYM)

c) .**CULPABLE**   **BLAMEWORTHY**

(SYNONYM)   (ANTONYM)

32 Insert the missing number.

9	16	12	21
18	32	24	42
27	48	36	63
36	64	48	

33 Insert the missing number.

6	
18	48

10	
8	36

14	
9	

34 Insert the number of the missing figure.

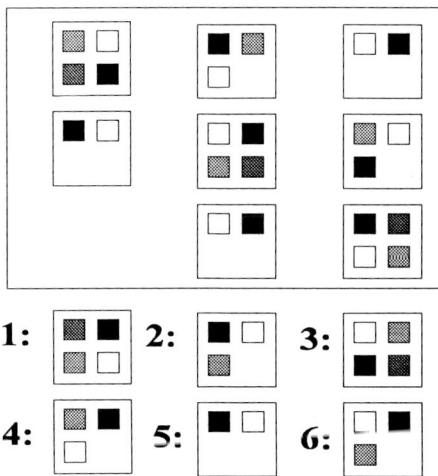

35 What is this anagram?

ANGLEMINT   (_____)

36 Insert the missing letters.

G   C   I   E   _   _

37 What is this anagram?

LEAFTRAWL   (_____)

38 Insert the missing numbers.

42   37   45   40   __   __

39 Insert the word that completes the first word and starts the second.

UNDER (____) AWAY

40 Using the key, insert the sum of the values surrounding each of the letters.

Key: ! = 6   @ = 7   # = 8

@	#	!	!	#
!	B	@	@	!
@	#	!	!	A
C	!	@	@	#

A: (   )   B: (   )   C: (   )

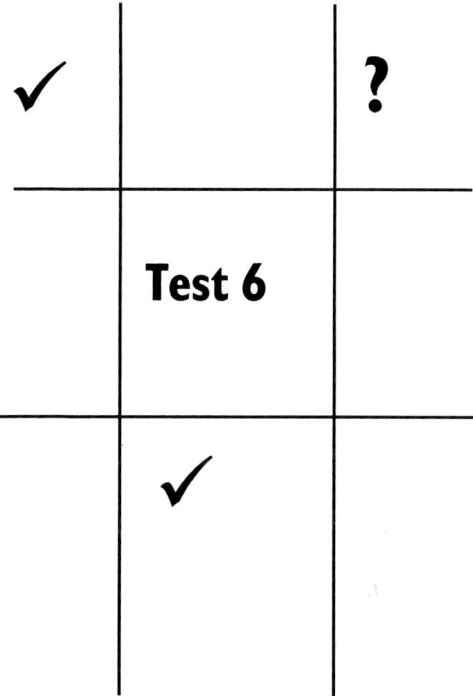

Test 6

1   What is this anagram?

CREAKRATE   (_____)

2   Insert the missing number.

15	5	10	16
18	6	12	8
3	21	12	6
8	12	10	

3   Underline the odd man out.

RUMBA

PANDA

TANGO

FANDANGO

JITTERBUG

4   Insert the missing number.

8   16   24   32   40   __

5   Insert the number of the missing figure.

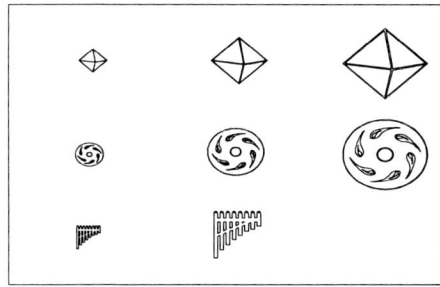

1:    2: 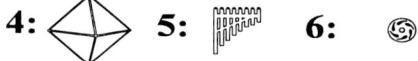   3:

4:    5:   6:

6   Insert the word that completes the first word and starts the second.

WALL (_____) WEIGHT

7   Insert the numbers to make the equation true.

4, 6, 7 and 8

(_ x _) - (_ x _) = 10

8   Insert the missing letter.

H   K   N   Q   T   _

9   Insert the missing number.

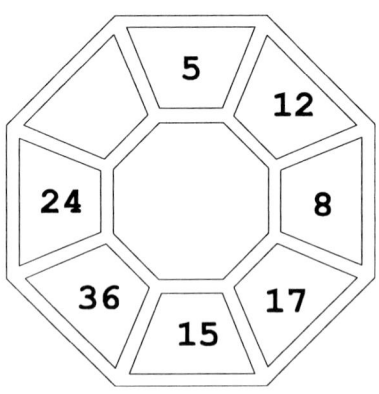

10   Insert the missing figure.

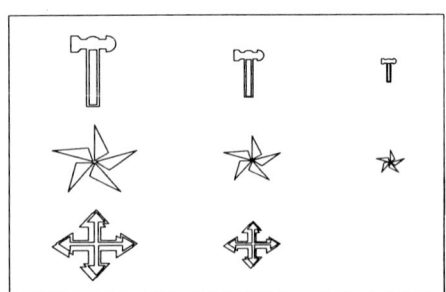

1:   **2:**   **3:**

4:   **5:**   **6:**

11   Insert the missing word.

16   9   (QUIP)   21   17

7   15   (____)   18   6

12   Underline whether each pair of words are SYNONYMS or ANTONYMS.

a) MYRIAD   **INNUMERABLE**

(SYNONYM)   (ANTONYM)

b) VISCOUS   **THIN**

(SYNONYM)   (ANTONYM)

c) HIATUS   **BREAK**

(SYNONYM)   (ANTONYM)

13   What is this anagram?

ACTSFAINT   (_____)

14   Insert word prefixed by the letters on the left.

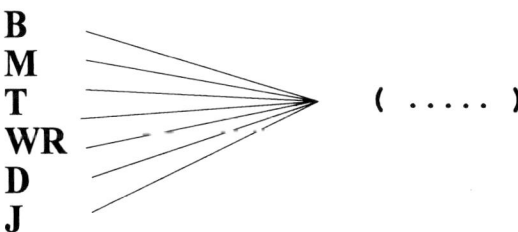

B
M
T
WR   (. . . . .)
D
J

15   Insert the missing letter.

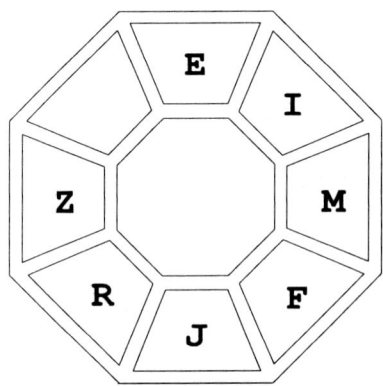

16   Insert the word that is a synonym for both of the other two words.

EMBED (   ) CABIN

17   Insert the missing word.

ES + (cloak) = (elude)

(   )

18   Insert the missing numbers.

9   18   27   __   45   __

19 Underline the two phrases that are the closest in meaning.

a) I take it in my stride.

b) They are over the moon.

c) We must look before we leap.

d) You are on cloud nine.

20 Insert the missing letter.

B   K   H   Q   N   _

21 Insert the missing number.

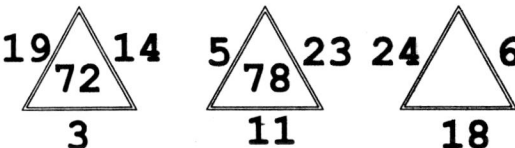

22 What is this anagram?

MISTMANGE   (_____)

23   Insert the number of the missing figure.

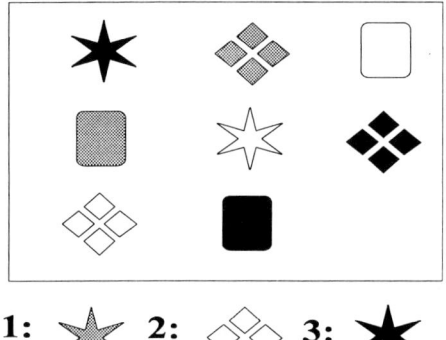

24   Insert the word that completes the first word and starts the second.

WOOD (_____) SHOP

25   Underline whether the final sentence is TRUE or FALSE.

All scooters are pelicans. Some pelicans eat wood but all like to play board games. All board game players have ten noses. Therefore all scooters have ten noses.

TRUE   FALSE

26   Insert the missing number.

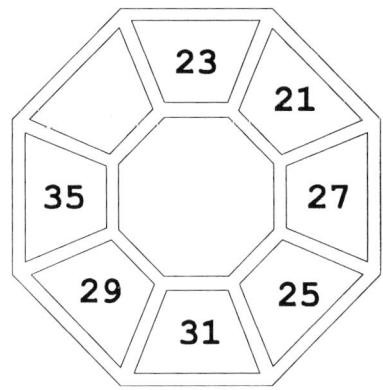

27   Insert the number of the missing figure.

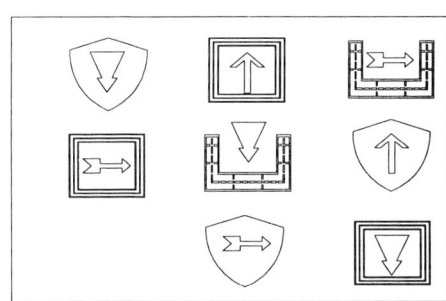

28   Underline the odd man out from 'schematic'.

SCHEMATIC: MAST, CHASE, MOST, CHIME, SHAM, TEAMS

29   Insert word suffixed by the letters on the right.

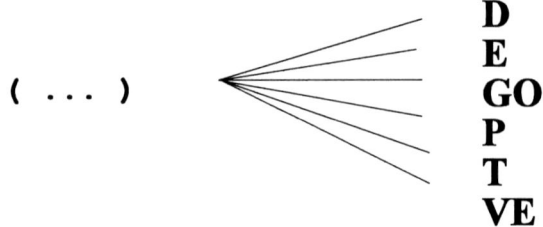

(...)

D
E
GO
P
T
VE

30   Insert the missing number.

5	
6	10

7	
9	21

12	
4	

31   Underline the odd man out.

MACAW

RAVEN

KESTREL

MAGPIE

MACKEREL

32 Insert the missing letters.

B   D   E   J   _   _

33 Insert the missing number.

18	12	10	3
43	8	3	17
25	5	6	5
34	23	3	

34 What is this anagram?

LAMBSRULE   (_____)

35 Insert the missing numbers.

23   46   30   60   __   __

36 Using the key, insert the sum of the values surrounding each of the letters.

<u>Key:</u>   % = 4   £ = 5   + = 9

£	N	£	+	£
+	%	£	%	+
%	£	M	+	£
+	£	%	%	L

L: (   )   M: (   )   N: (   )

37 Insert the word that is a synonym for both of the other two words.

WASTE (   ) DECLINE

38 Insert the missing letter.

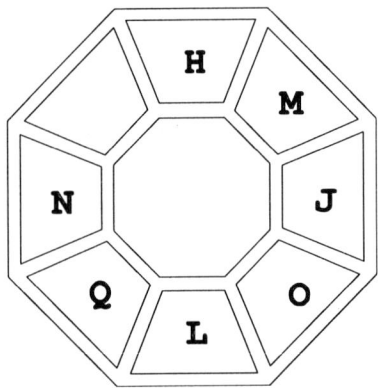

39 Insert the missing word.

IM + (tolerant) = (restless)

(   )

40 Insert the number of the missing figure.

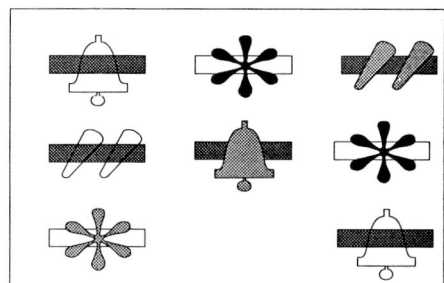

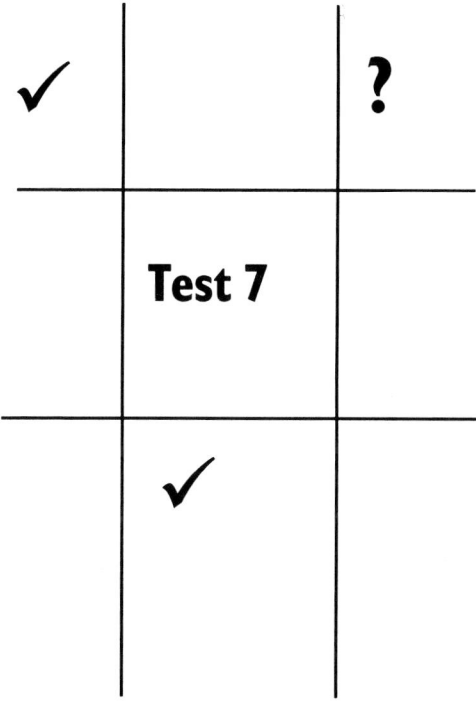

1 Underline the odd man out.

SQUARE

TRIANGLE

RECTANGLE

RHOMBUS

TRAPEZIUM

2 Insert the missing number.

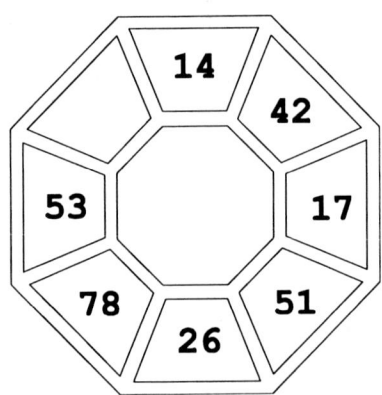

3 What is this anagram?

COATSLIDE (_____)

4   Underline whether the final sentence is TRUE or FALSE.

All elephants are socks. All socks are good guitarists, but most eat their instruments afterwards . Only bad guitar players pick fruit. Therefore some elephants pick fruit.

TRUE   FALSE

5   Insert the missing number.

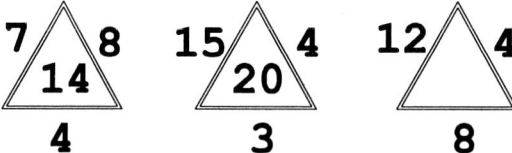

6   Insert the missing letter.

Z   _   P   K   F   A

7   Insert the missing number.

7   14   21   28   _   42

8   Insert the number of the missing figure.

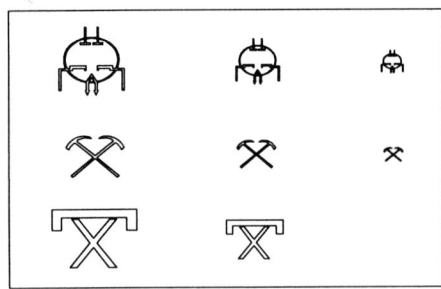

1: **2:** **3:**

4: **5:** **6:**

9   Insert the word that is a synonym for both of the other two words.

LEAP   (   )   RESTRICT

10   Underline the odd man out from 'travesty'.

TRAVESTY: RATE, START, VARY, STAVE, REST, CARVE

11   Insert the missing numbers.

14   28   _   56   _   84

12   Insert word suffixed by the letters on the right.

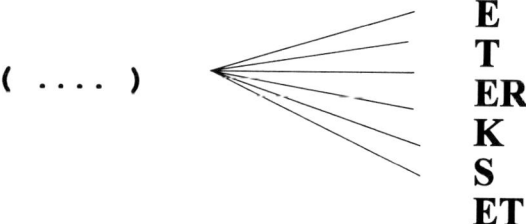

(....)

E
T
ER
K
S
ET

13   What is this anagram?

SONGSHUTE   (_____)

14   Insert the missing word.

S + (summit) = (utter)

(   )

15   Insert the missing numbers.

37   28   32   23   __   __

16 Insert the number of the missing figure.

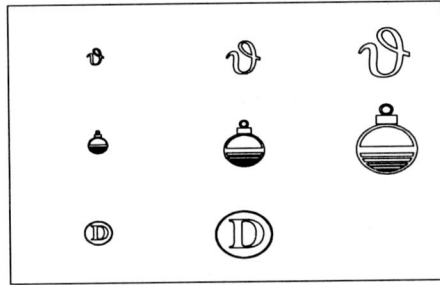

1: **2:** **3:** **4:** **5:** **6:**

17 Insert the missing letter.

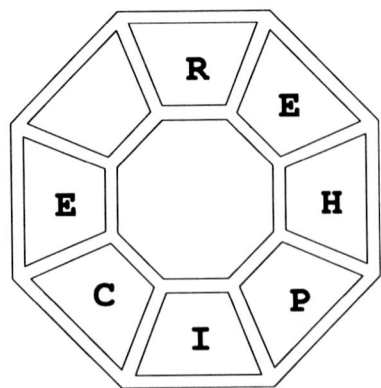

18 Insert the word that completes the first word and starts the second.

SAFE (_____) ROOM

19 Insert the numbers to make the equation true.

4, 6, 7 and 8

(_ + _) x (_ - _) = 30

20 Using the key, insert the sum of the values surrounding each of the letters.

Key: & = 3   ? = 9   ) = 12

?	&	X	)	&
)	)	&	?	)
&	Y	?	)	?
?	)	&	&	Z

X: (   )   Y: (   )   Z: (   )

21 Underline the two phrases that are the closest in meaning.

a) In the nick of time.

b) In the driving seat.

c) In total control.

d) In hot pursuit.

22 Insert the word that completes the first word and starts the second.

R + (expel) = (discard)

(   )

23 Insert the number of the missing figure.

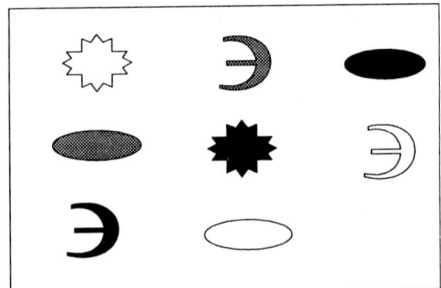

24 Insert the missing letter.

F   D   K   I   _   N

25 Insert the missing number.

24	12	6	3
56	28	14	7
16	8	4	2
72	36	18	

26 Insert the missing letters.

A   B   E   J   _   _

27 What is this anagram?

SEEDSNARE   (_____)

28 Insert the missing word.

16	13	(JUMP)	21	10
8	19	( )	9	23

29 Insert the missing number.

16	
8	4

6	
7	15

3	
18	

30 Insert the number of the missing figure.

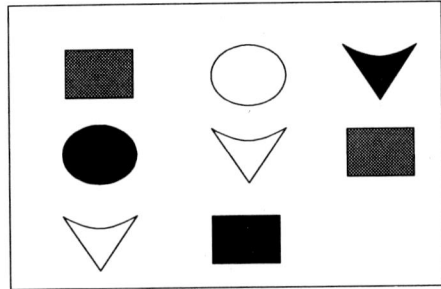

31 Insert the word that completes the first word and starts the second.

MORE (_____) SIGHT

32 Underline the odd man out.

ACE

KNAVE

DEUCE

JOKER

WIZARD

33 Insert the missing number.

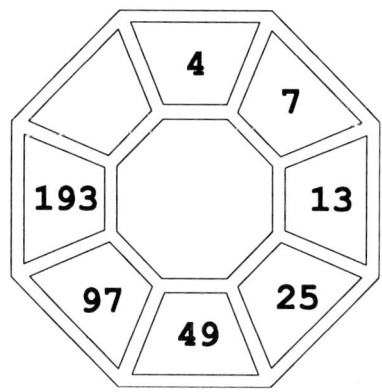

34 Underline whether each pair of words are SYNONYMS or ANTONYMS.

    a) **LUMINOUS**   **GLOWING**

       (SYNONYM)   (ANTONYM)

    b) **PIDDLING**   **TRIVIAL**

       (SYNONYM)   (ANTONYM)

    c) **ANALOGY**   **DISAGREEMENT**

       (SYNONYM)   (ANTONYM)

35   Insert word prefixed by the letters on the left.

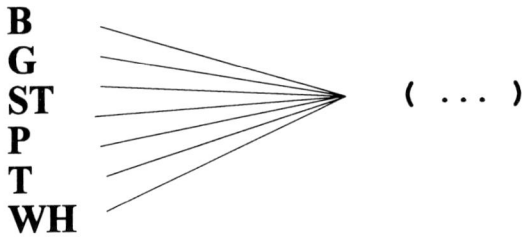

B
G
ST
P
T
WH

(...)

36   What is this anagram?

JADECIVET   (_____)

37   Insert the missing letter.

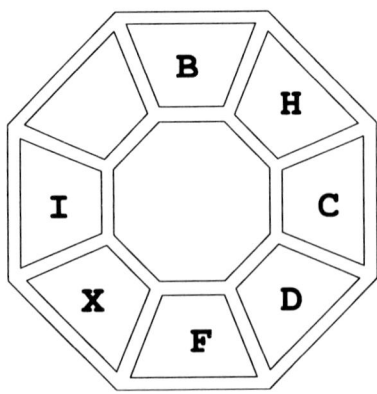

38 Insert the missing number.

12	24	36	48
6	12	18	24
17	34	51	68
19	38	57	

39 Insert a word that is a synonym for both of the other two words.

CONCEAL (   ) SKIN

40 Insert the number of the missing figure.

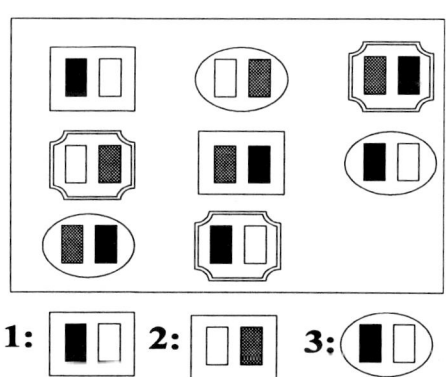

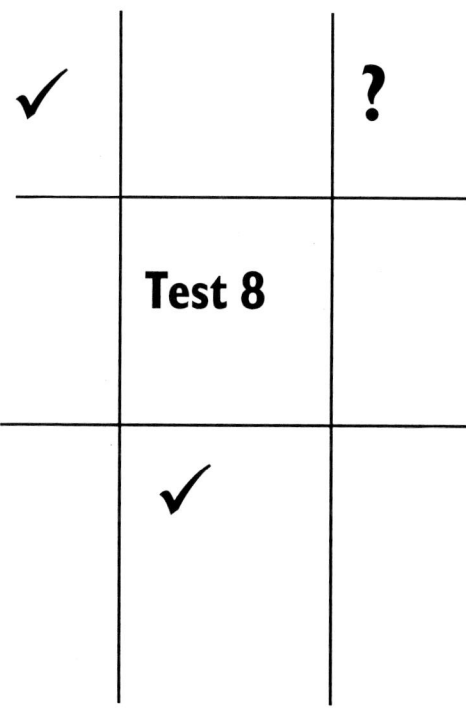

1   Insert the missing number.

88   72   56   40   (   )   8

2   What is this anagram?

DROWNFUEL   (   )

3   Underline the two phrases closest in meaning.

a) Making waves.

b) Splashing out.

c) In the heat of battle.

d) Causing trouble.

4   Insert the missing word.

ST + (scope)   =   (odd)

(   )

5   Underline the odd man out.

CONGREGATE: GROAN, RAIN, CRATE, GOAT, ANGER, NEAT

6   Insert the number of the missing figure.

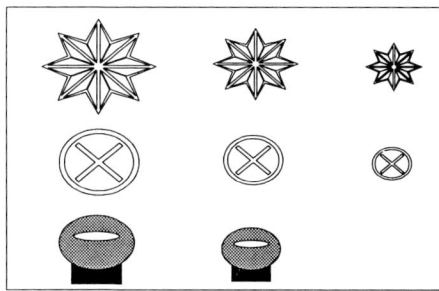

1: ⊗   **2:** ✷   **3:** 🥚

4: ✴   **5:** ●   **6:** ⊗

7   Insert the missing word.

20   1   (MOAT)   15   13

4   1   (   )   12   7

8   Insert the missing letter.

P   N   L   J   (   )   F

9   Insert the missing number.

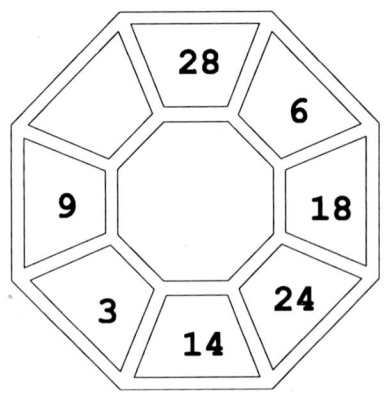

10   Insert the word that is a synonym for both of the other two words.

BOOK (   ) ORIGINAL

11   Insert the number of the missing figure.

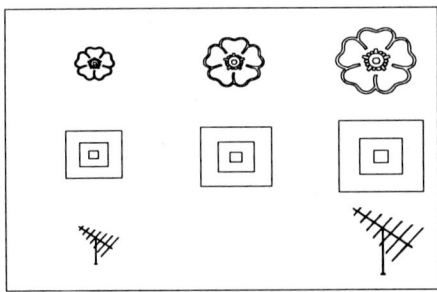

1:   **2:**   **3:**

4:   **5:**   **6:**

12 Insert the numbers to make the equation true.

4, 5, 8 and 9

(_ + _) x (_ - _) = 48

13 Insert the missing number.

9	12	15	14
6	8	10	26
8	3	1 1	28
32	4	( )	12

14 Insert the missing letter.

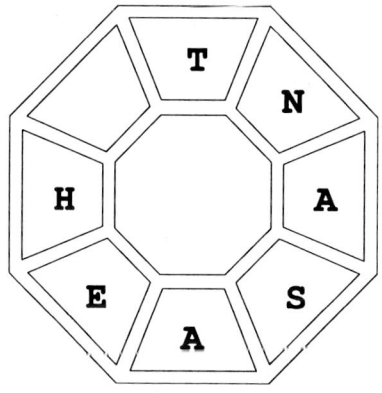

15 What is this anagram?

SNIDECOMA   (   )

16 Using the key, insert the sum of the values surrounding each of the letters.

<u>Key:</u> % = 4   £ = 6   & = 8

£	£	&	%	%
%	G	%	&	F
%	&	£	&	£
E	£	%	£	%

E: (   )   F: (   )   G: (   )

17 Insert the word that completes the first word and starts the second.

FLOOD (_____) HOUSE

18 Underline the odd man out.

HEARTS

DIAMONDS

SPANGLES

CLUBS

SPADES

19 Insert the missing numbers.

12 (   ) 34   45 (   )

150

20   Insert the missing letter.

    K   Q   M   (   )   O   U

21   Insert word prefixed by the letters on the left.

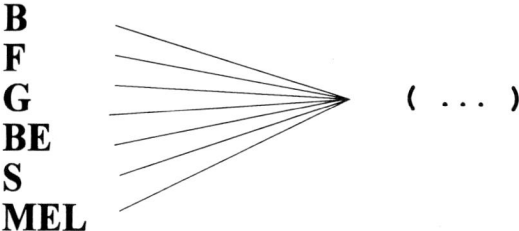

    B
    F
    G
    BE
    S
    MEL
                            (...)

22   Underline whether the final sentence is TRUE or
        FALSE.

        All goats are cars. Some cars are vegetarian, but all love jazz
        music. All jazz music lovers eat muesli for breakfast. Therefore
        all goats eat muesli for breakfast.

            TRUE   FALSE

23   Insert the missing numbers.

        18   9   14   7   (   )   (   )

24   Insert the number of the missing figure.

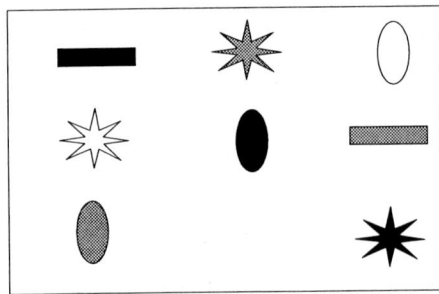

1: ▬ **2:** ⬭ **3:** ▭

4: ◯   **5:** ✳   **6:** ✳

25   Insert the missing number.

12	
3	18

5	
20	8

13	
15	

26   Insert the missing number.

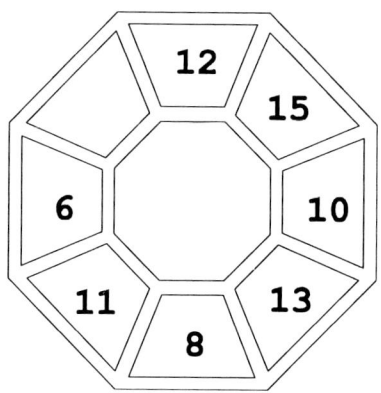

27   Insert the missing number.

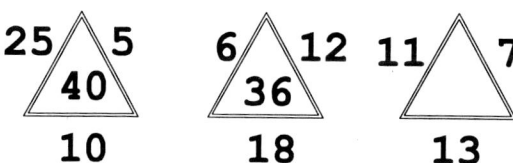

28   What is this anagram?

STEAMTIDE   (   )

29   Underline the odd man out.

FLOCK

SWARM

PRIDE

LITTER

SOLOIST

30   Underline whether each pair of words are SYNONYMS or ANTONYMS.

a) **HONEST**   **CROOKED**

(SYNONYM)   (ANTONYM)

b) **REALITY**   **FANTASY**

(SYNONYM)   (ANTONYM)

c) **PROLIFIC**   **ABUNDANT**

(SYNONYM)   (ANTONYM)

31   Insert the missing letters.

H   E   J   G   (   )   (   )

32 Insert the number of the missing figure.

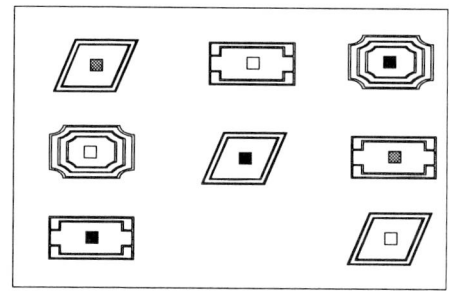

33 Insert the missing letter.

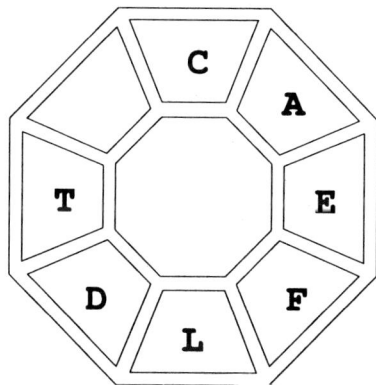

34   Insert the missing number.

16   5   9   20
 3   10   22   7
10   8   1   6
 8   14   ( )   4

35   What is this anagram?

TOOQUAINT   (   )

36   Insert the number of the missing figure.

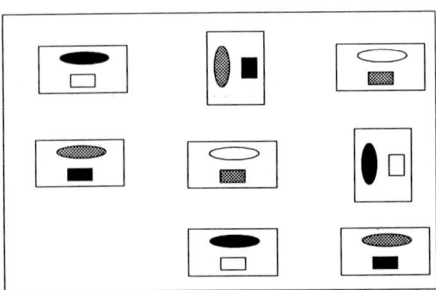

37 Insert the word that completes the first word and starts the second.

TIME (_____) MEAL

38 Insert word suffixed by the letters on the right.

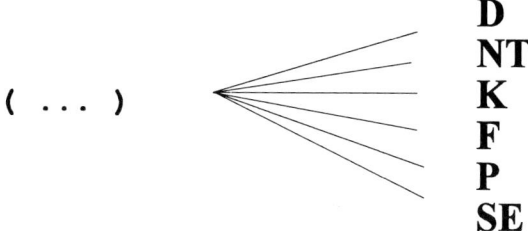

39 Insert the word that is a synonym for both of the other two words.

STUMBLE (   ) EXCURSION

40 Insert the missing word.

EX + (ordinary) = (justify)

(   )

Answers

Test I answers

1   5.

2   EACH.
Numbers show numerical position in the alphabet.

3   15.
Subtract 4 from previous number.

4   MOUSE.

5   18.
Opposites are doubles.

6   U.
Add 4 to previous letter.

7   4.

8   (5 x 4) - (6 + 3) = 11

9   b and d.

10   27. Middle = Left + Right + Bottom.
Middle = 9 + 13 + 5 = 27.

11   TREE.
The others are musical instruments.

12   51.
Add 9 to previous number.

13   D.
Word spells 'dinosaur' backwards.

14   SCHOOL.

15   J, V.
Add 4 to previous letter.

16   1.

17   6.
All rows add up to 24.
10 + 8 + 6 = 24.

18   FALSE.

19   a) SYNONYM.
b) ANTONYM.
c) SYNONYM.

20   11.
All numbers add up to 18:   5 + 2 + 11 = 18.

21   3.

22   KITE.

23   3.
Subtract 6 from previous number.

24   P = 30   Q = 46   R = 17.

25   CARTOON.

26   3, 81.
Triple the previous number.

27   a and c.

28   35.
Middle = (Left x Bottom) + Right.
Middle = (8 x 4) + 3 = 35.

29   Q, H.
     Subtract 3 from previous letter.

30   5.

31   3.
     Right = Top ÷ Bottom Left.

32   TRUE.

33   H.
     Opposites are doubles.

34   A = 20   L = 51   T = 37.

35   (3 + 5) x (9 - 8) = 8.

36   BROADWAY.
     The others are in London.

37   MONKEY.

38   3.

39   49, 22.
     Subtract 9 from previous number.

40   a) SYNONYM.
     b) SYNONYM.
     c) ANTONYM.

Test 2 answers

1   1.

2   (7 + 2) x (8 - 3) = 45.

3   43.
Add 7 to previous number.

4   a) ANTONYM.
b) SYNONYM.
c) ANTONYM.

5   b and d.

6   RIVER.

7   8.
Opposites are quarters: *32/4 = 8.*

8   L.
Subtract 3 from previous letter.

9   CARROT.

10   1.

11   5.
All columns add up to 38:   *20 + 13 + 5 = 38.*

12   TRUE.

13   DIAGONAL.
The others are on a compass.

14   27.
          Middle = Left - Right + Bottom
          Middle = 32 - 14 + 9 = 27.

15   DEAL.

16   5.

17   17.
          Subtract 6 from previous number.

18   G.
          Opposites are halves: N is 14 and 7 is G.

19   3.
          All numbers add up to 23.
          18 + 2 + 3 = 23.

20   C = 18   R = 21   Z = 48.

21   27.
          Middle = Left + Right + Bottom.
          Middle = 14 + 5 + 8 = 27.

22   WASP.

23   32, 8.
          Halve previous number.

24   2.

25   PENCIL.

26   34.
          Add 4 to previous number.

27   FALSE.

28   2.

29 51.
   Right = Top + Bottom Left.

30 a) ANTONYM.
   b) ANTONYM.
   c) SYNONYM.

31 ASTRONAUT.
   The others are from a circus.

32 Q, U.
   Add 2 to previous letter.

33 L.
   Word spells 'lemonade' backwards.

34 41, 27.
   Subtract 7 from previous number.

35 DRAGON.

36 $(3 \times 5) + (9 - 8) = 16.$

37 A = 21 C = 54 E = 35.

38 a and b.

39 P, A.
   Subtract 5 from previous letter.

40 5.

Test 3 answers

1   5.

2   15.
All columns add up to 32.

3   49.
Add 8 to previous number.

4   CLOCK.

5   BIRTHDAY.
The others are weekdays.

6   FACE.

7   W.
Add 5 to previous letter.

8   6.

9   6.
All numbers add up to 31.
12 + 13 + 6 = 31.

10   O.
Opposites are triples.
E is 5 and 15 is O.

11   FALSE.

12   36.
Opposites are triples.

13 c and d.

14 37.
Subtract 3 from previous number.

15 M = 27   P = 16   V = 42.

16 RECORD.

17 34.
Middle = (Left x Right) + Bottom.
Middle = (6 x 5) + 4 = 34.

18 2.

19 POSTER.

20 a) ANTONYM.
b) SYNONYM.
c) SYNONYM.

21 (8 - 5) + (7 x 2) = 17.

22 b and c.

23 4.

24 42.
Right = Top x Bottom left.
7 x 6 = 42.

25 FALSE.

26 18.
Subtract 8 from previous number.

27 VANILLA.
The others are fruits.

28 LEFT.

29   16, 64.
         Double the previous number.

30   O, U.
         Add 3 to previous letter.

31   FLIGHT.

32   3.

33   (6 - 5) + (3 x 4) = 13.

34   40.
         Middle = (Right + Bottom) x Left.
         Middle = (9 + 1) x 4 = 40.

35   J, F.

36   C.
         Word spells 'computer' backwards.

37   K = 36   U = 51   X = 20.

38   a) SYNONYM.
         b) ANTONYM.
         c) ANTONYM.

39   29, 65.
         Add 12 to previous number.

40   2.

Test 4 answers

1   3.

2   GRIP.

3   46.
Add 6 to previous number.

4   FINAL.

5   75.
Add 9 to previous number.

6   D.
Subtract 4 from previous letter.

7   GLOVE.
The others are worn on the feet.

8   21.
Middle = (Left - Right) x Bottom.

9   a and d.

10   4.

11   13.
All numbers add up to 28.

12   FALSE.

13   13.
Subtract 8 from the previous number.

14 a) SYNONYM.
     b) ANTONYM.
     c) SYNONYM.

15 $(6 + 3) \times (8 - 5) = 27$.

16 SAUCER.

17 R.
     Word spells 'relation' backwards.

18 1.

19 2. All rows add up to 27.
     $20 + 5 + 2 = 27$.

20 K = 51   L = 24   M = 18.

21 H, Q.
     Add 3 to previous letter.

22 CHEESE.
     The others are drinks.

23 RACKET.

24 6.

25 12.
     Middle = Left + Right - Bottom.
     Middle = 6 + 9 - 3 = 12.

26 TRUE.

27 A = 52   B = 35   C = 20.

28 27, 3.
     Each number is a third of previous one.

29 a) ANTONYM.

b) SYNONYM.
c) ANTONYM.

30 (2 x 8) + (9 - 7) = 18.

31 WISE.

32 YELLOW.

33 5.

34 C.
Opposites are quarters.
L is 12 and 3 is C.

35 b and d.

36 2.

37 21.
Right = Top - Bottom Left.

38 K, A.
Subtract 5 from previous letter.

39 7.
Opposites are halves.
14 ÷ 2 = 7.

40 17, 43.
Add 13 to previous number.

Test 5 answers

1 5.

2 18.
Add 6 to the previous number. 12 + 6 = 18.

3 INTERVALS.

4 GOTHENBURG.
This is not a capital city.

5 56.
Opposite numbers are doubles. 28 x 2 = 56.

6 ICE.

7 T.
Word spells 'TRIANGLE' backwards.

8 34, 102.
Add 17 to previous number.

9 6.

10 WASH.

11 O.
Add 4 to previous letter.

12 BAN.

13 a and c.

14 P.
Alternately subtract 3 and add 4.

15 MAZE.
Numbers show numerical position in the alphabet, in reverse.

16 72.
Middle = (Left - Right) x Bottom.
Middle = (14 - 2) x 6 = 72.

17 BRISK.

18 MIGHT.

19 1.

20 EXERCISED.

21 TRAIL.
There is no ' I ' in ELABORATE.

22 17.
All rows add up to 52.

23 CONDUCT.

24 (4 + 7) x (8 - 6) = 22.

25 5.

26 SCRAP.

27 26.
Alternately add 8 and subtract 4.

28 JADE.
The others are shades of red.

29   FALSE.
         No muffin can speak French.

30   J.
         Alternately subtract 4 and add 6.

31   a) ANTONYM.
         b) SYNONYM.
         c) SYNONYM.

32   84.
         Multiply first row by 2, 3 and 4 per column.

33   46.
         Add top to bottom and double for right.

34   6.

35   LAMENTING.

36   O, K.
         Alternately subtract 4 and multiply by 3.

37   WATERFALL.

38   48, 43.
         Alternately subtract 5 and add 8.

39   TAKE.

40   A = 34   B = 55   C = 21.

Test 6 answers

1   CARETAKER.

2   14.
     All columns add up to 44.

3   PANDA.
     The others are dances.

4   48.
     Add 8 to the previous number.

5   3.

6   PAPER.

7   (7 x 6) - (4 x 8) = 10.

8   W.
     Add 3 to the previous letter.

9   51.
     Opposites are triples.

10   1.

11   FROG.

12   a) SYNONYM.
     b) ANTONYM.
     c) SYNONYM.

13   FANTASTIC.

14 ANGLE.

15 L.
Opposites are doubles.

16 LODGE.
17 ESCAPE.

18 36, 54.
Add 9 to previous number.

19 b and d.

20 W.
Alternately add 9 and subtract 3.

21 96.
Middle = (sum of all numbers) x 2.
Middle = (24 + 6 + 18) x 2 = 96.

22 MAGNETISM.

23 1.

24 WORK.

25 TRUE.

26 33.
Alternately subtract 2 and add 6.
35 - 2 = 33

27 3.

28 MOST.
There is no 'O' in SCHEMATIC.

29 CAR.

30   16.
Right = (Top x Bottom) ÷ 3
Right = (12 x 4) ÷ 3 = 16.

31   MACKEREL.
The others are birds.

32   K, V.
Alternately double and add 1.

33   19.
Column 4 = Column 1 + column 2 ÷ column 3
19 = (34 + 23) ÷ 3

34   UMBRELLAS.

35   44, 88.
Alternately double and subtract 16.

36   L = 18   M = 40   N = 28.

37   REFUSE.

38   S.
Alternately add 5 and subtract 3.

39   IMPATIENT.

40   4.

Test 7 answers

1   TRIANGLE.
     The others have four sides.

2   159.
     Alternately multiply by 3 and subtract 25.
     53 x 3 = 159

3   DISLOCATE.

4   FALSE.
     No elephant picks fruit.

5   6.
     Middle = Left x Right ÷ Bottom.
     Middle = 12 x 4 ÷ 8 = 6

6   U.
     Subtract 5 from previous letter.

7   35.
     Add 7 to previous number.

8   4.

9   BOUND.

10   CARVE.
     There is no 'C' in TRAVESTY.

11   42, 70.
     Add 14 to the previous number.

12   PLAN.

13   TOUGHNESS.

14   SPEAK.

15   27, 18.
Alternately subtract 9 and add 4.

16   5.

17   D.
Word spells 'DECIPHER' backwards.

18   GUARD.

19   (8 + 7) x (6 - 4) = 30.

20   X = 39   Y = 63   Z = 24.

21   b and c.

22   REJECT.

23   6.

24   P.
Alternately subtract 2 and add 7.

25   9.
Divide columns by two along each row.

26   M, Z.
Alternately double and add 3.

27   SERENADES.

28   WISH.

29   7.
All numbers add up to 28.

30 2.

31 OVER.

32 WIZARD.
Others are names of playing cards.

33 385.
Add number to number - 1.
193 + (193 - 1) = 385

34 a) SYNONYM.
b) SYNONYM.
c) ANTONYM.

35 ALE.
36 ADJECTIVE.

37 L.
Opposites are triples.

38 76.
Add first column to subsequent columns.
57 + 19 = 76

39 HIDE.

40 2.

Test 8 answers

1　24.
Subtract 16 from previous number.

2　WONDERFUL.

3　a and d.

4　STRANGE.

5　RAIN.
There is no ' I ' in Congregate.

6　5.

7　GLAD.

8　H.
Subtract 2 from previous letter.

9　12.
Opposites are halves.
$24 \div 2 = 12$.

10　NOVEL.

11　1.

12　$(8 + 4) \times (9 - 5) = 48$.

13　2.
All rows add up to 50.
$32 + 4 + 2 + 12 = 50$.

14 P.
Word spells 'Pheasant' backwards.

15 COMEDIANS.

16 E = 18   F = 30   G = 46.

17 LIGHT.

18 SPANGLES.
The others are card suits.

19 23, 56.
Add 11 to previous number.

20 S.
Alternately add 6 and subtract 4.

21 LOW.

22 TRUE.

23 12, 6.
Alternately halve and add 5.

24 3.

25 5.
All numbers add up to 33.
13 + 15 + 5 = 33.

26 9.
Alternately add 3 and subtract 5.

27 31.
Middle = Left + Right + Bottom.
Middle = 11 + 7 + 13 = 31.

28 MEDITATES.

29   SOLOIST.
The others are group terms.

30   a) ANTONYM.
      b) ANTONYM.
      c) SYNONYM.

31   N, K.
Alternately subtract 3 and double.

32   4.

33   X.
Opposites are quadruples.
F = 6 and 24 = X.

34   5.
All columns add up to 37.

35   QUOTATION.

36   6.

37   PIECE.

38   LEA.

39   TRIP.

40   EXPLAIN.

IQ Conversion

IQ Conversion

Each test has 40 items, so your first task is to see how many you have got right, by checking with the answers given at the back of the book. The highest possible score is of course 40, but no child we tested got that high a score! Having got your score, you want to discover what IQ corresponds to it. To do that, consult Table 1 (for the younger children, 10–12, having done the first set of tests), or Table 2 (for the older children, 12–15, having done the second set of tests). Twelve-year-olds can do either set, or both. Very bright children who are younger than 10 can try the tests, but there is no table for them because for the younger children whom we tested we were unable to find a reliable IQ value for any given score.

Table 1

Score	Age		
	10	11	12
10	99	91	83
15	110	102	94
20	121	113	105
25	129	123	117
30	140	134	128
35	151	145	140

IQ rating

Table 2

Score	Age			
	12	13	14	15
5	109	100	96	93
10	119	109	105	102
15	130	120	114	112
20	140	131	126	123
25	149	140	135	132
30	160	149	144	141

 IQ rating

The scores are given in 5-point intervals, but intermediate values of IQ can be obtained quite easily. Taking examples from Table 2, for a 12-year-old, a score of 15 means an IQ of 130, a score of 20 means an IQ of 140. What about intermediate values? Take a score of 17 for a 12 year old. The score difference between 15 and 20 represents an IQ difference of 10 points. Therefore each point is worth 2 IQ points. A score of 17 would indicate an IQ of 130+ (2 × 2) = 134.

The test was geared to children with above-average IQs, so none are given for the most part for children with IQs below 100. There are two reasons for this. In the first place, IQ tests are constructed for selected populations. To make one for the general population means that the *accuracy* of measurement for a given amount of time is seriously decreased. If you target the 100 to 150 IQ group only, the accuracy of the measure is increased. The other reason is that experience shows that children (and parents) show an interest in books of this kind usually only when they have above-average IQs. We followed the same course with our adult tests.

The tests assume that the child has learned to read fluently, and to do simple sums. Unfortunately, not all schools nowadays provide the necessary teaching, and some bright youngsters may fail to do justice to themselves because of poor teaching. If your child does not do as well as you expect, this may be the cause. In any case, as we have said before, testing yourself can never give results as accurate as professional individual testing, so if you want to have a more precise estimate of your child's intelligence, consult an educational psychologist, and remember that as the children do the tests, their score will improve somewhat, because they are acquiring test sophistication; they are learning how to do IQ tests!